GW00482616

NETWORKS
ENGLISH FOR GCSE

written by

Paul Ashton
Jim Budd
Simon Fuller
Nikki Haydon
David Marigold
Jim Mulligan

edited by

David Marigold and Paul Ashton

ACKNOWLEDGEMENTS

Artwork by Lee Owen/Linden Artists

Illustrations reproduced by courtesy of BBC Hulton Picture Library (page 107), Collins Publishers (page 87), Donald Cooper (page 117), Leo Mason (page 10), Methuen (page 47), Robert Musson (page 17), National Portrait Gallery (page 35), Peter Newark's Western Americana (page 131), Popperfoto (pages 52 and 77), David Purdie (pages 93, 137 and 151), ROSPA (page 83), David Simson and Barnaby's (page 113), T. H. Williams and Barnaby's (page 24).

Extracts and poems are reproduced courtesy of the copyright holders: 'Hunger' and 'For the Fallen' by Laurence Binyon (Mrs Nicolette Gray and The Society of Authors on behalf of the Laurence Binyon Estate), 'The Radio Men' by Elizabeth Jennings (The Society of Authors), 'First Day at School' by Roger McGough (A. D. Peters), 'Digging for China' by Richard Wilbur from *Poems 1943–1956* (Faber & Faber), 'Arithmetic' by Carl Sandburg from *Complete Poems* (Harcourt Brace Jovanovich), 'A View of Things' by Edwin Morgan from *Poems of Thirty Years* (Carcanet Press), 'Florida Road Workers' by Langston Hughes (Pluto Press), *The Diary of Anne Frank* (Vallentine, Mitchell & Co), *The Secret Diary of Adrian Mole Aged 13¾* by Sue Townsend (Methuen), *Jenny: My Diary* by Yorick Blumenfeld (Penguin), *A Night Out* by Harold Pinter (Judy Daish Associates), 'Who's There?' by Arthur C. Clarke from *Of Time and Stars* (David Higham Associates), 'The Kiss' by Christine Purkis (Longman), 'The Emissary' by Ray Bradbury (Collins), 'The Flowers' by Alice Walker from *In Love and Trouble* (David Higham Associates), 'I Used to Live Here Once' by Jean Rhys from *Tigers are Better Looking* (André Deutsch), 'A Martian Sends a Postcard Home' by Craig Raine from *A Martian Sends a Postcard Home* (OUP), *A Sense of Freedom* by Jimmy Boyle (Canongate), *Black Boy* by Richard Wright (John Farquharson), *Memories, Dreams, Reflections* by Carl Jung (Collins), 'Discord in Childhood', 'Piano' and 'Snake' by D. H. Lawrence (Laurence Pollinger Ltd and the Estate of Mrs Frieda Lawrence Ravagli), 'Autumn Song' and 'View of a Pig' by Ted Hughes (Faber & Faber), untitled poem on p. 141 by Brian Lee, leaflet by the Research Defence Society, *Buddy* by Nigel Hinton (J. M. Dent), 'In Memory of my Grandfather' by Edward Storey (Robert Hale), 'Song of the Battery Hen' by Edwin Brock (Martin Secker & Warburg Ltd), 'KBW' by Farrukh Dhondy from *The East End at Your Feet* (Macmillan). Every effort has been made to contact copyright holders, but we will be pleased to rectify any omissions in future printings.

First published 1989
by John Murray (Publishers) Ltd
50 Albemarle Street, London W1X 4BD

Typeset by Pioneer Associates, Perthshire
Printed by The Bath Press, Avon

British Library Cataloguing in Publication Data

Networks.
  1. English language — For schools
  I. Marigold, David
428

ISBN 0-7195-4361-4

CONTENTS

Introduction About this Course and the GCSE   4

UNIT 1   Snapshots: Developing Views of Characters   7

UNIT 2   Sweet and Sour: Writing Poems   14

UNIT 3   Keeping a Record: Diaries and Journals   31

UNIT 4   Writing Dialogues: Script-writing   41

UNIT 5   Brief Lives: Working on Short Stories   51

UNIT 6   Writing for Your Rights: Running a Campaign   79

UNIT 7   The Professionals: Studying an Author   85

UNIT 8   Futures: Decision-making and Simulations   96

UNIT 9   Life Story: Autobiography   106

UNIT 10   *Macbeth*: Studying a Play   116

UNIT 11   Behind the Words: Explaining Poems   129

UNIT 12   My Opinion is . . .: Points of View   143

UNIT 13   On the Rack: Writing for a Magazine   151

UNIT 14   The Play in the Book: Script-writing   156

UNIT 15   Close Encounters: Thinking about Poetry   162

UNIT 16   The Incident: Writing and Race   178

Advice on writing Developing Your Written Work   190

INTRODUCTION
ABOUT THIS COURSE AND THE GCSE

What is it?

Networks is organised into self-contained units. They can be taken in any order.

Each unit has opportunities for talking, reading, and writing to help you cover your GCSE course. All the units are relevant to your English syllabus, and some of them can be directly useful if you are also studying for English Literature.

How you will be assessed for GCSE

Your school will have made the decision about what form your exam will take. You will certainly be assessed in some of the following ways:

Written coursework

This means that by the end of your course you will be expected to present a folder which contains a selection of your best writing. So, most of the writing you do at school and at home will be important to your final grade. It is possible that the whole of your exam will be based on your coursework folder.

Oral coursework

Your teacher (and possibly other teachers) will keep track of your contribution and progress when you are involved in discussion situations. Your oral work will normally take place in your ordinary English lessons, but you may have special sessions at some times during the two years of the course. It is important that you get used to working together to develop your skills in talking as well as your written English.

Written exam paper

Your assessment may be based on a combination of course work and an exam paper. The paper will be taken towards the end of your course. It is impossible to revise 'facts' for English. They don't exist.

The only real way to prepare for an exam paper is gradually to develop your reading and writing skills during your time at school and at home.

What will be assessed?

The teachers who listen to you talk or who read your writing will be hoping that you can demonstrate certain strengths in English.

1. Variety of forms

Can you handle a variety of written *forms*? The forms could include letters, poetry, essays giving opinions and information, stories, reports and reviews, playscript etc. This does not mean that you are expected to be equally good at all of them, but you should be prepared to tackle more than just one or two.

2. Style

Can you write in *styles* which are appropriate in different situations? You will need to consider whether the language and tone are suitable for the people (audience) reading your work, and whether the style is right for the purpose of the writing.

3. Rules

Can you be reasonably accurate in using the rules of written language? You should continue to develop your ability to spell, punctuate, and to use paragraphs. These rules are needed to help the readers of your work to follow the sense of what you say. Needless to say, clear handwriting is important for it to be read at all!

There is some general advice on developing your writing on pages 190–192.

4. Speech

Can you communicate well when you talk? You must be prepared in group discussion to express your ideas and to be reasonably clear in what you say. This does not mean that what you say will be judged as right or wrong, but whether you are prepared to

▶ speak your mind,
▶ to consider what's said to you before replying,

▶ co-operate and contribute to the work of the group.

You will probably have the chance to give short talks to a group of friends or to the class. You will be assessed on your ability to give clear opinions and explanations, and to communicate successfully with your audience.

5. Reading

Can you demonstrate in discussion and in writing that you can understand and respond to what you read? This might range from leaflets and newspapers to poetry and complete novels. On the one hand you may be asked to analyse closely the meanings and language in a piece of print; on the other you may have to imagine and use your own experiences to appreciate some of the main themes and issues in literature.

What the symbols mean

The symbols below are used throughout the book to indicate which kind of activity is involved at each stage.

| Talking | Writing | Talking and writing |

| Role play/acting | Research | Formal talk/performance |

Networks will help you, not only in your GCSE course, but also to develop your skills so that you can use them for your own pleasure and purposes.

We also hope that some of the units will help you to explore ideas and issues which are important in themselves, so that your English course will be interesting as well as useful to you.

DAVID MARIGOLD
PAUL ASHTON

SNAPSHOTS

DEVELOPING VIEWS OF CHARACTERS

Views of characters

We all see people in different ways, different lights. This depends, in part, upon our relationship with them. You see your dad or mum differently from the way their friends see them. It also depends upon personality. There are some people we get on with better than others. We are not equal friends with everyone!

By taking a number of different people's views of someone, we can build a picture of what they are like.

Read the following views of a sports personality.

Has Leonie quit at twenty-five?

Temperamental sports star Leonie Rogers appears to have left the sport which made her a legend and a millionaire but could not make her happy.

We attempt to piece together the extraordinary and contradictory character of superstar Leonie by talking to those who knew her best: her mother, her teachers, her friends and her many enemies. How could one person be so generous and charming yet also childish, spoilt and vindictive?

▶ *Her mother*

'I'm very proud of Leonie. Everything she has achieved has been through hard work. She was always prepared to practise longer than anyone else. When she was young Leonie was a happy child; always out playing with her friends, never sad. She's very generous: for instance, as soon as she'd earned enough money she bought me a new house. At that time she had no car of her own and few clothes but she insisted on me having a new place. She said I'd had a hard life and now deserved some comfort.

I've heard about the rows in restaurants, read in newspapers that she's mean with her money, that she can't take defeat and so on. I don't believe these stories. It's just the press trying to sell more newspapers. At first Leonie could do no wrong, the press called her 'Lionheart', now they're happy to attack her for the slightest thing!'

▶ *A schoolfriend*

'I'm not surprised that things have gone wrong for Leonie. We used to be close friends in the old days, used to walk to school together and all that sort of thing. But as soon as Leonie became famous and started to win tournaments, she dropped all her old friends. I'm not bitter but it's a shame. She never replied to letters, and when I called her on the phone she was never in, though I knew she was.

I suppose when I look back it was always that way. Always me who got in touch. Unless Leonie wanted me to do something, then I'd hear from her soon enough! Still we were good friends and had some great times together.'

▶ The headteacher of Leonie's old school

'I couldn't say that Leonie was a model pupil for her tennis commitments meant that she was away from school a great deal. It was obvious from the time Leonie arrived at the school that she had a gift for tennis. Though she had this great natural ability, Leonie was prepared to put in long hours practising, which is often unusual in very gifted players. Even at twelve years old, she was very ambitious and determined to win major tournaments like Wimbledon.

Inevitably I suppose Leonie wasn't able to or didn't wish to make similar efforts with her academic work. She left school with few qualifications.

Leonie was sociable and even-tempered. I find many of the stories I read in the press about her hard to believe. They must be exaggerated. However it must be very difficult to cope with the pressure of all the media attention; always in the public eye with no real private life. Mind you she's played some wonderful tennis over the past few years. I always enjoy watching her play — she moves so very gracefully.'

▶ Her manager

'Leonie quitting tennis! You've got to be joking! She's just in need of a few weeks rest and some quiet practising. Wants to spend time improving her serve. This last year's been especially busy, played in all the major tournaments and won two of them! You can't be on peak form all the time. She's still got her tremendous appetite for the game.

Difficult to work with — absolute nonsense! Very considerate and dedicated more like. Newspapers have got it all wrong just like when they blow up disagreements on court. I see a brief exchange of words and a couple of gestures during a match. Next day it's blazing headlines. Given the pressures on top tennis players, I think Leonie is very level-headed and relaxed.'

▶ A journalist

'It is fashionable to blame the press when a player has problems. While I have some sympathy for Leonie Rogers, I must say she has brought most of her troubles on herself. She made herself good copy for newspapers; the arguments on court, being seen in fashionable night spots with the latest man in her life, going over the top at press conferences and so on. You name it, Leonie's done it. Now it's all gone sour so the bad old press gets the blame again.

Tennis players complain about the pressure but who would work on an assembly line for a hundred pounds a week if they were able to earn thousands playing tennis in the sun?'

▶ A neighbour

'I was an admirer of Leonie Rogers until she moved in next door two years ago. I'd thought of her as a kind, friendly person. I soon realised my mistake. She's always having dreadful arguments with her boyfriends and she doesn't care how much noise she makes. I remember one time, late in the evening it was, she actually attacked a boyfriend's car with a hammer! And the language! I've never heard anything like it, talk about fish wives! We had to call the police in the end.

If it's not arguments then it's wild all-night parties. I thought she was supposed to be an athlete. She doesn't get up until the late afternoon and then stays up half the night. I'm not surprised she's been losing a lot recently. Success seems to have gone to her head.

Fortunately she is away a lot but when she's away there's the dogs. The house is guarded by these three ferocious Dobermans. I'm sure they're not fed properly for they howl all night long.

We've tried to raise these matters politely with Miss Rogers but we had only abuse in return. Now we're taking her to court.'

▶ A tennis rival

'I've played against Leonie since she was sixteen. She's always a tough opponent to beat. She's become famous for her scenes and arguments with umpires. Her anger is directed at officials when they make silly mistakes, like saying a ball is out when it's clearly in. What makes Leonie even angrier is that they never seem to admit they are wrong. I mean anyone can make a mistake, so why not admit it! When she's playing badly, Leonie gets furious with herself; she's been playing very poorly recently; her confidence has gone. Mind you Leonie never takes it out on her opponent.

I hope Leonie hasn't quit tennis, that she is just going through a bad patch. It would be such a shame to lose a great player. It's hard to stay keen after ten years on the circuit. When you're not playing you're travelling or practising. Never in one place for more than two weeks. Makes having a private life almost impossible. So there comes a point, especially when you've won plenty of tournaments and made enormous sums of money, when you think to yourself, why go on?'

Different points of view

Do the characters who talk about Leonie give you any hint of what they themselves are like? This activity will help you to analyse what they reveal about themselves.

There are seven characters who give their views of Leonie.
▶ Work in pairs or threes.
▶ Call yourselves A, B and C.

▶ Each choose a different character from amongst the seven.

▶ Study your characters to assess what they seem like and what seems to be motivating their view of Leonie.

▶ When you have done this, imagine that B and C are radio reporters who have asked A the question, 'What is Leonie really like?'

▶ A should read the text to B and C in such a way as to bring out the tone and feelings which might lie behind his/her chosen character.

▶ After the first reading, B and C should advise A whether any improvements could be made or what was particularly convincing.

▶ B and C should then follow the same activity.

▶ If available, a cassette tape recorder would be useful to listen to your reading.

Sympathetic and unsympathetic

A few weeks pass and it is formally announced that Leonie Rogers has retired from international tennis. As Leonie is a sports superstar, there are a number of newspaper articles following her shock retirement. Some are friendly and sympathetic, while others are hostile and unsympathetic.

▶ Your next activity is to write two newspaper articles about Leonie, one that is sympathetic and one that is not.

▶ Use the information you have already been given and invent more if you need. If you want to write about her career in detail, you may need to find out the names of the major tennis tournaments — ask people in your class, your sports teachers, or try the library.

▶ Opposite is a newspaper article to remind you how they are set out.

Edgy Charlton are almost up

CHARLTON ATHLETIC, the club that nearly died are on the point of promotion to the First Division.

They need just a draw from their last two games to be absolutely certain of returning to the top flight after an absence of 29 years.

By BARRY FLATMAN
Charlton 2   Fulham 0

But failure was not in anybody's mind as the fans, who used to suffer at The Valley and sweated as Charlton came within 30 minutes of extinction two years ago, danced with delight in their new shared home at Selhurst Park.

Even manager Lennie Lawrence, who refuses to rejoice until promotion is a mathematical certainty, accepted the adulation of the thousands who chanted his name in triumph.

'I cannot stop the celebrations but we will keep going until the very end of our last game against Wimbledon,' said Lawrence.

Struggle

'Their manager, Dave Bassett is my best friend in the game and I sincerely hope Wimbledon do well — but when they come here we will do our best to turn them over.'

For nearly 70 minutes nervous Charlton struggled to land the goal that would open the door to the First Division.

Rock-bottom Fulham, already doomed to the Third Division, fought a brave rear-guard action and Charlton's young winger Mark Stuart squandered three glorious scoring chances.

Notice the use of 'Edgy' Charlton, not just Charlton.

Dramatic background.

Name of Reporter.

Quotes from the manager and his name given.

Story broken up into small paragraphs.

Sub-headline catches your eye and further breaks up the print.

Frequent use of descriptive words.

Four 'snapshots'

Now some 'snapshot' suggestions for you to try. Read through the four ideas below and choose one of them. Continue to work with at least one other person in your class to talk over your ideas before tackling the writing.

1. The shoplifter

The facts

On 12 November seventeen-year-old _____ _____ was sentenced to two years for a series of shoplifting offences. These had all occurred over the past two years. _____ was stopped by store detectives outside Robinson and Jones, the department store. £500 worth of jewellery was found on the youth. It was estimated at the trial that _____ had stolen nearly £10,000 worth of goods in the two-year period.

▶ What do people think of this shoplifter?
▶ Give the views of at least four of the following people. (Remember, they may have sharply contrasting pictures of the seventeen-year-old.) Imagine they are speaking to the magistrate at _____'s trial.

 The mother/father of the young person
 Store detective at Robinson and Jones
 Police officer who made the arrest
 Their form teacher
 Their headteacher
 A friend/childhood friend
 Their employer/career's officer
 A workmate.

2. The runaway

What led _____ to run away from home?

▶ Think of a situation which would persuade someone that they have to leave home. Now make a list of people who were involved and whose points of view will make the reasons for _____ running away clearer. He/she is one person you will probably want to include.

▶ Imagine they are speaking to a social worker. It would help to enact this in role play before writing the snapshots.

The runaway's story

Imagine how _____ came to leave home. Focus on the last ten or fifteen minutes *before* they leave, and the first hour *after* they leave. You might want to write in the first person. Remember that this is likely to be a time of mixed emotions for them — so that it's important not just to give details of what they do, but also their thoughts and feelings.

3. Snapshots of a famous person

Write four different snapshots of a pop/rock star, television personality, a famous woman, a politician . . . Remember that we are often only shown one side of a personality's character. Your snapshots could broaden this out.

4. Use snapshots as a basis for a story

Write snapshots of a character created by you, and use it as a basis for a story or a playscript.

Literature

You can use this 'snapshot' technique for talking and writing when you are studying a novel, short story, or play. You can:
▶ Invent some characters to provide a variety of views about a particular character in a story.
▶ Use other characters (even very minor ones) who appear in the narrative to give written reports, or write letters or diaries in which they reveal information and give opinions about the character you have chosen to analyse.

It's always worthwhile to try this technique out with your friends through role play or improvisation before writing.

SWEET AND SOUR

WRITING POEMS

2

This unit contains a collection of poems.

Each section provides you with ideas to write your own poetry, and help for you to decide how to write them.

You aren't expected to work your way through this unit all at once. You might try one section then come back to others later on.

I am . . .

Hunger

I come among the peoples like a shadow.
I sit down by each man's side.

None sees me but they look on one another
And know that I am there.

My silence is like the silence of the tide
That buries the playground of children;

Like deepening of frost in the slow night,
When birds are dead in the morning.

Armies trample, invade, destroy,
With guns roaring from earth and air.

I am more terrible than armies,
I am more feared than cannon.

Kings and chancellors give commands;
I give no command to any,

But I am listened to more than kings
And more than passionate orators.

I unswear words and undo deeds.
Naked things know me.

I am the first and last to be felt by the living.
I am hunger.

Laurence Binyon

'Hunger' is written as though hunger is alive and can speak like a person. This technique is called personification.

Performing

Can you speak this poem in such a way as to bring out the powerful and sinister character of Hunger?

Perhaps a group could make a tape recording or give a performance in which lines spoken could be allocated to different people, or some lines could be spoken together in a chorus.

Composing your own poetry

Write a poem which uses personification.

You could choose one of these as your 'speaker':

sleep	fear	pain
laughter	fire	rain
wind	love	television

Or you could choose one of your own.

When I was little

The radio men

When I was little more than six
I thought that men must be
Alive inside the radio
To act in plays, or simply blow
Trumpets, or sing to me.

I never got a glimpse of them,
They were so very small.
But I imagined them in there,
Their voices bursting on the air
Through that thin, wooden wall.

Elizabeth Jennings

First day at school

A millionbillionwillion miles from home
Waiting for the bell to go. (To go where?)
Why are they all so big, other children?
So noisy? So much at home they
must have been born in uniform
Lived all their lives in playgrounds
Spent the years inventing games
that don't let me in. Games
that are rough, that swallow you up.

And the railings.
All around, the railings.
Are they to keep out wolves and monsters?
Things that carry off and eat children?
Things you don't take sweets from?
Perhaps they're to stop us getting out
Running away from the lessins. Lessin.
What does a lessin look like?
Sounds small and slimy.
They keep them in glassrooms
Whole rooms made out of glass. Imagine.

I wish I could remember my name
Mummy said it would come in useful.
Like wellies. When there's puddles.
Yellowwellies. I wish she was here.
I think my name is sewn on somewhere
Perhaps the teacher will read it for me.
Tea-cher. The one who makes the tea.

Roger McGough

Digging for China

'Far enough down is China,' somebody said.
'Dig deep enough and you might see the sky
As clear as at the bottom of a well.
Except it would be real — a different sky.
Then you could burrow down until you came
To China! Oh, it's nothing like New Jersey.
There's people, trees, and houses, and all that.
But much, much different. Nothing looks the same.'

I went and got the trowel out of the shed
And sweated like a coolie all that morning,
Digging a hole beside the lilac-bush,
Down on my hands and knees. It was a sort
Of praying, I suspect. I watched my hand
Dig deep and darker, and I tried and tried
To dream a place where nothing was the same.
The trowel never did break through to blue.

Before the dream could weary of itself
My eyes were tired of looking into darkness,
My sunbaked head of hanging down a hole.
I stood up in a place I had forgotten,
Blinking and staggering while the earth went round
And showed me silver barns, the fields dozing
In palls of brightness, patens* growing and gone
In the tides of leaves, and the whole sky china blue.
Until I got my balance back again
All that I saw was China, China, China.

Richard Wilbur

*dishes or plates

Work in a group

1. Read 'The Radio Men', 'First Day at School', and 'Digging for China'.

All three poems are about small children inventing explanations in order to make sense of the world.

Discuss which of the three poems you prefer.

2. Tell each other, and make a list, of the things you believed when you were little.

Often these will consist of things adults said, like 'Eating your cabbage will make your hair nice and curly'. Or will be answers to questions you asked yourself, like 'Where does the food go once you've swallowed it?', or 'What are clouds made of?'

3. Use anything from the list to write a poem on this idea. Roger McGough wrote his as if a small child is thinking, whereas Elizabeth Jennings and Richard Wilbur present their poems as memories. You could try either style.

Arithmetic

Arithmetic is where numbers fly like pigeons in and out of
    your head.
Arithmetic tells you how many you lose or win if you know
    how many you had before you lost or won.
Arithmetic is seven eleven all good children go to heaven —
    or five six bundle of sticks.
Arithmetic is numbers you squeeze from your head to
    your hand to your pencil to your paper till you get the
    answer.
Arithmetic is where the answer is right and everything is
    nice and you can look out of the window and see the
    blue sky — or the answer is wrong and you have to start
    all over again and try again and see if it comes out this
    time.
If you take a number and double it and double it again
    and then double it a few more times, the number gets
    bigger and bigger and goes higher and higher and only
    arithmetic can tell you what the number is when you
    decide to quit doubling.
Arithmetic is where you have to multiply — and you carry
    the multiplication table in your head and hope you
    won't lose it.
If you have two animal crackers, one good and one bad,
    and you eat one and a striped zebra with streaks all
    over him eats the other, how many animal crackers will
    you have if somebody offers you five six seven and you
    say No no no and you say Nay nay nay and you say
    Nix nix nix?
If you ask your mother for one fried egg for breakfast and
    she gives you two fried eggs and you eat both of them,
    who is better in arithmetic, you or your mother?

Carl Sandburg

Maths lesson rules

Always subtract bottom from top.
A plus and a plus equals a minus
or, a plus depending on the month
equals circumference but
equals fruit and pastry depending on the lesson.
Don't blow bubbles.
Remember to write who you love on desks
Don't eat the chalk
Come to lessons.
Don't sit on chairs — sit on the floor (it's safer).
Enter cupboards at your own risk.
Try to avoid flirting with new maths books.
Skive when possible. Don't get caught.
Look interested — in what's going on outside.
Cheat in exams.
Don't scribble rude words on the board
write them clearly.
Never go to detentions, or other dishonourable functions.
Don't pluck your eyebrows — save that for geography.
Christine Bates
Jill Etheridge
Steyning

Here poets have each made a funny poem out of something that's usually thought of as serious — maths. Could you do the same? You'll have to try to look at one of your school subjects, or lessons, in a new way, to bring out the funny side.

▶ Suppose one of the plants or animals in a biology lesson started speaking? Or a teacher became confused, and started getting everything mixed up?

▶ What about a list of do's and don'ts like the one in 'Maths lesson rules', which was written by two girls in a school?

▶ Or a list of possible disasters in a lesson, starting with 'what if . . . ?'

Mindvoice

VOICE 1: Imagining things, lying here.
No lights to protect me from
Imagining things.

VOICE 2: What's that?

VOICE 1: It's nothing. If I tell myself
It's nothing
Then I won't see anything.

VOICE 1: Wish I hadn't watched the ghost film.

VOICE 2: I always say that.
I lie here and think.

VOICE 1: What if I wake up
And there's someone staring
Straight into my face?

VOICE 2: Oh, go to sleep.

VOICE 1: What's that shape
Stepping out of the wardrobe?

VOICE 2: It's nothing.
Go under the covers
Like a fish
Disappearing under water after quickly
Catching air.
Stay here. I think.
It can't get you here.
I think.

Kim Walker
15 years, Walworth School

In her poem Kim Walker has used the idea of two voices in her head having a conversation. When you think about it, a lot of our thinking is carried on in this way, especially when we are trying to make a decision or to prepare ourselves for something important.

In the first draft she wrote Kim didn't pay any attention to *how* she was going to arrange the lines; she wrote quickly to get her ideas and words down. For instance, the last section was originally written like this:

> Go under the covers like a fish disappearing
> under water after quickly catching air. Stay
> here, I think, it can't get you here.

Then she simply decided to make shorter lines which she thought *felt* and *looked* more interesting. She didn't do it according to any special rules.

Your own 'Mindvoice' poem

You will first have to choose an interesting situation like:
▶ waiting to be punished
▶ deciding to make a complaint
▶ wondering if a friend still likes you
▶ working up courage to ask for something.

Write your ideas and words out quickly, and then decide how you are going to organise them. You can use Kim's layout of 'Mindvoice' if it's helpful.

What I love/what I hate

A view of things

what I love about dormice is their size
what I hate about rain is its sneer
what I love about the Bratach Gorm is its unflappability
what I hate about scent is its smell
what I love about newspapers is their etaoin shrdl*
what I hate about philosophy is its pursed lip
what I love about Rory is his old grouse
what I hate about Pam is her pinkie
what I love about semi-precious stones is their preciousness
what I hate about diamonds is their mink
what I love about poetry is its ion engine
what I hate about hogs is their setae
what I love about love is its porridge-spoon
what I hate about hate is its eyes

*these are the letters that occur most often in the English language in order of frequency.

what I love about hate is its salts
what I hate about love is its dog
what I love about Hank is his string vest
what I hate about the twins is their three gloves
what I love about Mabel is her teeter
what I hate about gooseberries is their look, feel, smell, and taste
what I love about the world is its shape
what I hate about a gun is its lock, stock, and barrel
what I love about bacon-and-eggs is its predictability
what I hate about derelict buildings is their reluctance to disintegrate
what I love about a cloud is its unpredictability
what I hate about you, chum, is your china
what I love about many waters is their inability to quench love

Edwin Morgan

List poems

This is an easy form for writing a poem. What counts is the
strangeness of the loves and hates — the fact that they're
unpredictable and surprising.

Try your own version. The things can be true or made up. You can
put in things that only mean something to you — other people don't
have to understand everything. You could mix many different things
together, as Edwin Morgan does, or write just about people, or about
school . . .

Contrasts

Swift things are beautiful

Swift things are beautiful:
Swallows and deer,
And lightning that falls
Bright veined and clear,
Rivers and meteors,
Wind in the wheat,
The strong-withered horse,
The runner's sure feet.

And slow things are beautiful:
The closing of day,
The pause of the wave
That curves downward to spray,
The ember that crumbles,
The opening flower,
And the ox that moves on
In the quiet of power

Elizabeth Coatsworth

 In 'Swift things are beautiful', the poet mentions eight swift things, and five slow things. Can you do the same, and arrange them in two groups?

There are other contrasts you could choose:

heavy/light   rough/smooth
light/dark   shiny/dull
happy/sad   sweet/sour

The poet has rhymed every other line. You can try to do the same, or make your own poem unrhymed.

Questions

Many poems are organised as a series of questions and answers.

Sea, sand and sorrow

What are heavy?
Sea, sand and sorrow.

What are brief?
Today and tomorrow.

What are frail?
Spring blossoms and youth.

What are deep?
The ocean and truth.

Christina Rossetti

 You could use this structure for a poem of your own. You might want to use Christina Rossetti's questions — but supply different answers.

Or make your own questions from a collection of adjectives — like tall, cold, grey etc.

Over the page is a more complicated poem about the devastation caused by the war in Vietnam.

What Were They Like?

1. Did the people of Vietnam
   use lanterns of stone?

2. Did they hold ceremonies
   to reverence the opening of buds?

3. Were they inclined to quiet laughter?

4. Did they use bone and ivory
   jade and silver, for ornament?

5. Had they an epic poem?

6. Did they distinguish between speech and singing?

1. Sir, their light hearts turned to stone.
   It is not remembered whether in gardens
   stone lanterns illumined pleasant ways.

2. Perhaps they gathered once to delight in blossom,
   but after the children were killed
   there were no more buds.

3. Sir, laughter is bitter to the burned mouth.

4. A dream ago, perhaps. Ornament is for joy.
   All the bones were charred.

5. It is not remembered. Remember,
   most were peasants; their life
   was in rice and bamboo.
   When peaceful clouds were reflected in the paddies
   and the water buffalo stepped surely along terraces,
   maybe fathers told their sons old tales.
   When bombs smashed those mirrors
   there was only time to scream.

6. There is an echo yet
   of their speech which was like a song.
   It was reported their singing resembled
   the flight of moths in moonlight.
   Who can say? It is silent now.

Denise Levertov

Object

Probably all of us have a few special objects in our lives. Occasionally our memories are jogged or our feelings are stirred by them.

The poem 'Peace' is an example of this.

It was being asked to think about a clock that reminded Gill Callen of the death of a member of her family, and of her own feelings towards time and death.

Peace

Last Sunday evening after tea
A bird of paradise flew over a blue ocean
And in through the open window.
It settled on the mantlepiece amongst
Brown wrinkled faces of the past
And a clock ticking future moments
Into present.
It told me there is a happy land.

Three days ago it rained,
A blackness drumming on the pavement,
The air stiff with cold.
People hurried on, stone-faced.
I hurried on, too, towards home
And opened a window.

I watched the rain, and soon
A bird of paradise flew over a blue ocean
And in through the open window.
It settled on the mantelpiece amongst
Brown wrinkled faces of the past
And a clock ticking future moments
Into present.
It told me there is a happy land.

At first light this morning someone close
Died.
I sat up and watched the clock ticking
And the wrinkled faces
Who must have felt this way before,
Not sad but desolate.
An empty room full of empty photographs.
I sat and thought

And soon a bird of paradise,
A bird of peace,
Flew over the blue oceans of my thoughts
And in through the open windows of my mind
And settled among remembered faces
And a clock ticking through my life.
It told me there is a happy land.

Gillian Callen (15)

Your own memory poem

Is there a particular object in your life which has special memories? A toy? A record or photograph? Or even a piece of furniture or a book?

Write a poem about it — either a description or the memories associated with it.

Worth shouting about?

Poetry has always been used as one of the ways to protest about injustice in the world.

Langston Hughes is a black American poet whose poem focuses on the difference between rich and poor. He wrote it in the 1950s when there was massive racial discrimination in the southern states of the USA.

Florida Road Workers

I'm makin' a road
For the cars
To fly by on.
Makin' a road
Through the palmetto thicket
For light and civilization
To travel on.

Makin' a road
For the rich old white men
To sweep over in their big cars
And leave me standin' here.

Sure,
A road helps all of us!
White folks ride —
And I get to see them ride.
I ain't never seen nobody
Ride so fine before.
Hey buddy!
Look at me.
I'm makin' a road.

Langston Hughes

Otto Castillo lived in Guatemala. From 1954 to 1967 he belonged to a political movement trying to overthrow the military dictatorship which governed his country. After arrest, he was tortured before execution. He was thirty-one years old.

His poem is a promise to fight to free his country from the army colonels who have abolished democracy.

Let's Take a Stroll

Let's take a stroll Guatemala,
I'm coming along with you.

I'll go down as far as you want me to.
I'll drink from the same bitter cup.
I'll use my eyes so you can see again
I'll give you my voice so you can sing
I'll die to give you life.

I'm tired of crying about you.
Now I'll walk with you.
Together we'll make the sparks fly!
I'll work with you,
Help you to do things — because
I am part of you
Born here one October to face the world.

O Guatamala,
We must tear the roots
From those colonels who piss
On your walls. We'll hang them up

On a tree where the violet dew
Shimmers with the people's anger.

I will go with you.
I will go always with the peasants
And the workers and with any one
Who loves you.

Let's start the journey, my country.
I'm coming with you.

Otto Castillo

Poems expressing your own opinions

What have you got to say about the world you live in? Your feelings and opinions are as valuable and as important as anyone else's.

What are the real issues for you? Are they big ones — like war, starvation, politics, discrimination, cruelty to children or animals? Or maybe there's something more personal to you that makes you really angry.

What is your poem going to sound like? Will it be for shouting out loud — like 'Florida Road Workers'? Or will it be quiet and angry and intense?

3

KEEPING A RECORD

DIARIES AND JOURNALS

Hence this diary. In order to enhance in my mind's eye the picture of this friend for whom I have waited so long, I don't want to set down a series of bald facts in a diary like most people do, I want this diary to be my friend, and I shall call my friend Kitty.

(From *The Diary of Anne Frank*)

This unit is about the way people, real or imaginary, keep a record of what has happened to them.

Making notes

Part of this unit requires you to keep a diary on recent events in your life. (Keeping brief notes on what you do over the next three days, *starting now*, would be useful preparation for this activity.)

Diaries and journals

Many people keep a diary. Most of the time it's to remind us that we are going to a party on Saturday night or are due to visit friends next weekend, making sure we don't forget Nan's birthday or go away when we have arranged for friends to come and see us!

Below is an example of a diary which records what is *due to happen in the future*. It looks as though it is written in code. It is obviously not intended to be published.

AM	PM	Thursday **13**
Buy — cereals — onions — grapes	Terry coming in to work — 2.15?	
Phone John this evening — about car.	Poss. go to meeting on charity organizations	

AM	PM	Friday **14**
Go in late — take kids to school.	Annie W. 01- 886 4121 — has information about concert.	
11.30 Take car in for oil — change		
7.30 Ruth's party. Buy something to take.		

However some people keep a record of events *that have already happened.*

This record will vary because people have different reasons for keeping a diary and different interests. It can vary from recording details of what they ate for lunch (egg, beans, and chips again) to details of what happened in government.

It is this record of the past that we shall be looking at in this section.

Here are five extracts from very different diaries or records, which show why some people keep diaries.

Logbook

Log Narrative: 30 May. Channel 14 [Harwich Harbour Radio] was alive with traffic — and this was the busiest time with ferry boats in and out. Several boats were lost in the fog and the skippers of large vessels were concerned. Because of this I radioed Harwich and gave my position and explained that I would keep outside the dead water channel. We found Cliff Foot Buoy — which seemed easy after Pye End. As we arrived there the *Princess Beatrix* slipped out of the fog inward bound from Hook of Holland. In the next 45 minutes *Prinz Hamlet, Dana Anglia*, and other lesser vessels glid past, almost silently.

It seemed prudent to anchor while all this was happening. Miraculously as we rode comfortably to anchor visibility improved for the first time and I could see Shotley Spit and Langard Point buoys in the opposite directions. Our careful, first-time navigation in dense fog — over 27 miles — was over. It had been a fascinating experience and the product of good team-work and clear decision-making.

So — as we felt pleased with ourselves — we tried to raise anchor, only to find we had snagged a laid chain. With a bit of ingenuity we luckily came free of it and then set off on our journey to Wolvestone. We radioed Harwich to report our final movement. Bob took the helm up the Orwell — a lovely evening.

1 June. In torrential rain we motored up the Orwell, under the magnificent bridge and up to Fox Marina for the boat. After a dusty welcome, we moored alongside, and spent the day at the drop of the anchor — in the main shipping channel (but with no vessel movement) — while I changed the plugs and then sailed back to Wolvestone — where there was a cosmopolitan atmosphere as the first of the Dutch and Belgian boats arrived for their summer holidays. After a leisurely look round the huge variety of boats we were early to bed in readiness for an early start in the morning to catch the two hours of ebb tide.

 Do you know anyone who keeps a record of facts about an activity or interest?

The next extract is from the diary that thirteen-year-old Anne Frank kept for much of the Second World War. Anne and her family were Jews who lived in Amsterdam. For two years the family hid, to escape persecution, in sealed-off rooms in an office block. Eventually the Germans found them. Many of Anne's family died in concentration camps. Anne herself died of typhus in Belsen in 1945.

The extract was written after they had been hiding for about five weeks. 'Kitty' is the name she gave to her diary.

Diary

Friday, 21st August

Dear Kitty,

The entrance to our hiding place has now been properly concealed. Mr Kraler thought it would be better to put a bookcase in front of our door (because a lot of houses are being searched for hidden bicycles), but of course it had to be a movable bookcase that can open like a door. Mr Vossen made the whole thing. We had already let him into the secret and he can't do enough to help. If we want to go downstairs, we first have to bend down and then jump, because the step has gone. The first three days we were all going about with masses of lumps on our foreheads, because we all knocked ourselves against the low doorway. Now we have nailed a cloth filled with sawdust against the top of the door. Let's see if that helps!

I'm not working much at present; I'm giving myself holidays until September. Then Daddy is going to give me lessons; it's shocking how much I've forgotten already. There is little change in our life here. Mr Van Daan and I usually manage to upset each other, it's just the opposite with Margot whom he likes very much. Mummy sometimes treats me just like a baby, which I can't bear. Otherwise things are going better. I still don't like Peter any better, he is so boring; he flops lazily on his bed half the time, does a bit of carpentry and then goes back for another snooze. What a fool!

It is lovely weather and in spite of everything we make the most we can of it by lying on a camp-bed in the attic where the sun shines through an open window.

Yours, ANNE.

'In spite of everything . . .'

▶ How is Anne feeling at this stage?
▶ What clues are there to suggest problems in the future?
▶ Does giving her diary a name make a difference to the way Anne writes?

Samuel Pepys

This is from the diary of Samuel Pepys, written in London in 1661. He was twenty-nine years old at this time.

He kept a diary for many years, recording details of his family life, his loves, his work, people he knew and met, hundreds of details of small and great things that interested him.

6th. Home to my father, who could discerne that I had been drinking, which he did never see or hear of before: so I eat a bit of dinner, and then took horse for London, and with much ado, the ways being very bad, got to Baldwick. There lay, and had a good supper by myself. The landlady being a pretty woman, but I durst not take notice of her, her husband being there. Before dinner, I went to see the church, which is a very handsome church. I find that both here and everywhere else that I come, the Quakers do still continue, and rather grow than lessen.

7th. Called up at three o'clock, and was a-horseback by four; and, as I was eating my breakfast, I saw a man riding by that rode a little way upon the road with me last night; and he, being going with venison in his panyards to London, I called him in, and did give him his breakfast with me; and so we went together all the way. At Hatfield, we bayted and walked into the great house through all the courts; and I would fain have stolen a pretty dog that followed me, but I could not, which troubled me. To horse again, and by degrees with much ado got to London, where I found all well at home, and at my father's, and my Lady's, but no newes yet from my Lord where he is.

8th. (Lord's day.) To church, and coming home again, found our new mayd Doll asleep, that she could not hear to let us in, so that we were fain to send a boy in at a window to open the door to us. Begun to look over my accounts, and, upon the whole, I do find myself, by what I can yet see, worth near £600, for which God be blessed.

9th. To Salisbury Court play-house, where was acted the first time, ''Tis pity shee's a W——e,' a simple play, and ill acted, only it was my fortune to sit by a most pretty and most ingenious lady, which pleased me much. . . .

10th. This morning come the mayde that my wife hath lately hired for a chamber-mayde. She is very ugly, so that I cannot care for her, but otherwise she seems very good. To the Theatre — 'The Merry Devill of Edmunton,' a very merry play, the first time I ever saw it, which pleased me well.

11th. To Dr Williams, who did carry me into his garden, where he hath abundance of grapes: and he did show me how a dog that he hath do kill all the cats that come thither to kill his pigeons, and do afterwards bury them; and do it with so much care that they shall be quite covered; that if the tip of the tail hangs out, he will take up the cat again, and dig the hole deeper, which is very strange; and he tells me, that he do believe he hath killed above 100 cats.

12th. In the afternoon had notice that my Lord Hinchingbroke is fallen ill, which I fear is with the fruit that I did give them on Saturday last at my house; so in the evening I went thither, and there found him very ill, and in great fear of the small-pox.

13th. I went out to Charing Cross, to see Major-General Harrison hanged, drawn, and quartered; which was done there, he looking as cheerful as any man could do in that condition. He was presently cut down, and his head and heart shown to the people, at which there was great shouts of joy. It is said, that he said that he was sure to come shortly at the right hand of Christ to judge them that now had judged him; and that his wife do expect his coming again. Thus it was my chance to see the King beheaded at White Hall, and to see the first blood shed in revenge for the King at Charing Cross. Setting up shelves in my study.

 Is Pepys's diary of any interest to us, over 300 years later? What use can be made of it in our century?

Even from this short piece, what impression do you get of:
▶ life in London in the 1660s
▶ the personality and interests of Pepys?

Fictional diaries

The following extracts are both fictional. The first is taken from *The Secret Diary of Adrian Mole Aged 13¾* by Sue Townsend. The second is from *Jenny: My Diary*, kept by a fictional character who survives a nuclear attack on Britain. Both books want to give the impression that they were written by Adrian and Jenny.

The Secret Diary of Adrian Mole

Thursday April 16th

Got a birthday card from my Auntie Susan, two weeks late! She always forgets the right day. My father said that she's under a lot of pressure because of her job, but I can't see it myself. I'd have thought that being a prison wardress was dead cushy, it is only locking and unlocking the doors after all. She has sent a present via the GPO so with luck I should get it by Christmas. Ha! Ha!

Friday April 17th
GOOD FRIDAY

Poor Jesus, it must have been dead awful for him. I wouldn't have had the guts to do it myself.

The dog has mauled the hot-cross buns; it doesn't respect any traditions.

Saturday April 18th

Got a parcel from Auntie Susan. It is an embroidered toothbrush holder and it was made by one of the prisoners! She is called Grace Pool. Auntie Susan said that I should write and thank her! It is bad enough that my father's sister works in Holloway Prison. But now I am expected to start writing to the prisoners! Grace Pool could be a murderess or anything!

Still waiting for the eleven pounds eighty pence. It doesn't seem as if my mother is desperate to see me.

Sunday April 19th
EASTER SUNDAY

Today is the day that Jesus escaped from the cave. I expect that Houdini got the idea from him.

My father forgot to go to the bank on Friday so we are penniless. I had to take the pop bottles back to the shop to buy myself an Easter egg. Watched film, then had a fantastic tea at grandma's. She made a cake covered in little fluffy chicks. Some of the fluff got into my father's mouth, he had to have his back thumped hard. He always manages to spoil things. He has got no Social Decorum at all. Went to see Bert Baxter after tea. He was pleased to see me and I felt a bit rotten because I have neglected him lately. He gave me a pile of comics. They are called the *Eagle* and they have got great pictures. I read them until 3 a.m. this morning. Us intellectuals keep anti-social hours. It does us good.

Jenny: My Diary

WEDNESDAY

Wanted to go to the hairdresser before work today, but early – before breakfast – Gerard told me to keep the kids home. He took the train and tube to Metal Box. Too risky to go by car, he said. All incredibly upsetting. Everyone continually glued to TV and the radio. He called from work at 10·30 and told me to start packing the Volvo. The PM issued a national emergency declaration... the UK might be at war in a few hours. Are these the final words I'll write? Got to pack right now... Thank God Bill and Simon are home...

SUNDAY? MONDAY?

Arrived at the shelter at about 1·30 Pryce was guarding the entrance with the shotgun. He bade us welcome and told us to unload the Volvo before parking it at some distance away. Ronald Trakin and Lester Pinder helped to get it all out.

There was nothing in our "apartment" except what we had brought in the Volvo and the sleeping bags. Everyone was watching the TV set in the communal dining room.

The Prime Minister declared war at 3pm. Ten minutes later missiles were falling all over England and the TV reception stopped. Nobody knows what blast waves rocked this island. We didn't feel much at all. Two families apparently tried to make their way into the shelter, but Pryce shot them in cold blood. He was terribly upset. I think he has suffered a nervous breakdown.

I wanted to get out, but Trakin argued that I had to stay for the children. I didn't want to be trapped in a tomb without my husband. Don't know what happened after that, but I guess I became violent and someone (Trakin?) just knocked me out.

Woke up to the cries of the children:
"We're locked in and Daddy's outside".

Why do you think these two writers chose to use the diary format for these stories? What advantages were there in writing this way? Do you think there were also disadvantages?

Slices of life

Choose either (1) or (2).

1. Record, in brief, the main events that happened to you during the last three days. Then choose two or three of these events to write about in more detail.

2. Look back over the past few months and jot down what you can remember. (Things that happened at home, at school, successes, failures, disappointments, films you saw, sports you played or watched, friends you met, arguments you had, places you've been.)

Now write a journal of these months. You won't want to include everything, just those things that seem most important to you.

You might want to organise it month by month:
▶ 'Usually November is really boring. This year it was really great/good . . .'
▶ 'June's been awful. For a start it's rained all the time. For another . . .'
▶ 'December, that's Christmas time . . .'

Or you could organise it under headings such as Family, Sport, School, People, Places, Hobbies etc.

Writing stories using the diary format

It is possible to tell stories, as well as recording real events in your life, through a series of entries in a diary. The last two extracts were fictional diaries that told the story of Adrian Mole and what happened to Jenny after a nuclear attack.

Some suggestions for creating a fictional diary or journal

Remember — when you write *you* will be the character you have invented. Choose one of these suggestions.
1. Diary of a holiday. Maybe a holiday where everything went wrong — food awful, hotel not finished, beach miles away, missed flight, car broke down etc. Or a holiday that turned out in an unexpected way.
2. Tell the story of a friendship through a series of diary entries. This could be a friendship that came to an end or could be of one that continues.

3. Week in the life of: a detective, nurse, sports person, long-distance lorry driver, rock/pop star, journalist, teacher, unemployed person, someone you know well. Concentrate on a typical week in their working lives.

4. Diary of a school journey. Either one you have been on in the past or an invented one.

5. Journal of an old person looking back on two or three moments of great happiness or sadness in his or her life.

6. You are a crew member on the proposed Space Mission STS — +40. One of your jobs is to keep a diary or log book of the flight for one week. This diary may include diagrams and sketches.

This is a difficult task, so the ideas below are to help you.

Before you start to write your space log book, record, or diary, there are a number of things you need to think about:
▶ Where is the flight going to? Is it due to orbit the Earth, or to explore the solar system?
▶ In what century will this be set?
▶ How long is the flight expected to take?

Other points you could think of to help make your diary interesting:
▶ feelings at take-off/landing
▶ space sickness
▶ experiment that goes wrong or a malfunction in a piece of equipment
▶ communication with Earth
▶ names of the crew? Do all the crew get on with each other?
▶ are there animals/insects on board?
▶ daily routine
▶ what can you see during your flight?

7. Write a humorous diary-day for an eccentric character. Choose your own — but if you are stuck for ideas you can use one of these:
▶ a girl who hates animals
▶ a person who is obsessed with looking in mirrors
▶ a person who fears electrical gadgets
▶ a boy who keeps losing things.

4

WRITING DIALOGUES

SCRIPT-WRITING

In this unit you will be asked to play out the roles of people in a variety of situations and to turn spoken activities into written playscripts.

Conversation break

The playscript below has blank spaces where Tony's dialogue should be.

Working in pairs, read through the whole script first, and then discuss what Tony might have said.

Make a rough draft of his words. You will be coming back to make changes to them later in the activity.

DIANE: Hi, Tony. Haven't seen you for ages. Going anywhere special?
TONY:
DIANE: I might as well go with you. Got to pick up my magazine from the paper shop.
TONY:
DIANE: Not likely! That'll be the day you catch me carrying shopping for a boy.
TONY:
DIANE: Are you going to the fifth-year disco on Friday?
TONY:
DIANE: Who with?
TONY:
DIANE: Oh. I hope you know what you're doing. I mean, you have seen her dance, haven't you? Like a chicken in splints.
TONY:
DIANE: All right, no need to get offensive.
TONY:
DIANE: Well I was going out — but my dad's being awkward about staying out. Ten-thirty, he says. Isn't that stupid? Things are just getting moving by then, and he expects me to leave. I dunno. It's not worth my while going if I have to leave that early.
TONY:
DIANE: Midnight! How did you get round your mum?
TONY:

DIANE: Stop a second. I'll just dodge in here and get my mag. Oh no! I've left my money at home. Tony . . . er . . . you couldn't lend me fifty pence, could you?

TONY:

DIANE: O.K. I'll carry your shopping. But it better not be heavy stuff.

Getting started

 Still in pairs, go through the scene again and discuss and make notes on:

▶ what Tony and Diane might look like (description of characters)

▶ where their conversation takes place (setting the scene)

▶ the places in the dialogue where the characters might make certain movements, or do things, or use a certain change of voice, or where they might pause or be silent for a while (stage directions).

 Use your notes to help you to write the complete script. You will have to turn your discussion ideas into the final words to be used by actors. The script should be organised in the following way:

▶ set the scene

▶ character descriptions

▶ write the dialogue copying Diane's and making a final draft of Tony's. *As you do this* insert any stage directions which would help the actors.

 Finally, ask two people in your class to act out your script. Make any changes suggested by them, if you think they will improve it.

Extra ideas

 It would be best to discuss this work in pairs before writing your individual versions.

1. Continue the playscript of the conversation between Diane and Tony. Remember to include any change of scene and the stage directions.
2. Make a playscript of a conversation between Diane and her dad as she tries to persuade him to let her stay late at the disco.
3. Act out any one of the scripts you write:
   ▶ either as a radio piece (using a tape recorder)
   ▶ or as a reading for a rehearsal of the scene
   ▶ or as a live performance.

Changing roles

In the first section, Tony and Diane talk easily and naturally because they know each other well and are the same age. In other words, they are of an equal status.

However, this is not the case for many situations in which we have to make conversation.

It is likely that we behave differently (play a different role), according to *what* the situation is and *who* we are talking with.

Playing different roles

Work in two sets of pairs — X and Y, A and B. X and Y will do the role play. A and B will be observers to give opinions later.

1. One of you be Person X, the other Person Y.
   X and Y are close friends.
   The situation is that yesterday, during a visit, X accidentally spilt/broke and damaged something in an old person's house.
   X tells Y about the incident.
   Y must listen carefully, and then ask any questions for further information.
2. Repeat the activity — only this time Y plays the role of the old person whose property was damaged.
3. A and B compare the two dialogues. Discuss whether X behaved differently and spoke in a different way when talking to the old person.
4. X and Y write the playscript of the conversation between X and the old person.
   Try to write it so that it sounds as close to the real speech you used when you were doing it out loud.
   ▶ Give both of them names
   ▶ Set the scene
   ▶ Describe the characters
   ▶ Lay the dialogue out in playscript form
   ▶ Include any stage directions or instructions to the actors which would help to direct them how to show feelings and the way to speak.
5. A and B can act out the playscript written by X and Y. Do changes need to be made?

Two by two

It is 4.30 p.m. on Monday. Since leaving school for the day three schoolfriends have been sitting in a local café, drinking coffee.

The owner comes to their table and asks them to leave. He says they have been sitting too long and accuses them of noisy behaviour. One of the group refuses to leave, and the owner attempts to pull him/her out of the seat.

There is a small scuffle and some crockery is knocked from the table and is smashed.

The police are called, and ten minutes later the local beat officer arrives.

Acting a scene

 This incident will form the basis for a series of conversations.

It would be best to work in pairs, but you could be in a group of three or four if you wanted to change from dialogues to more than two characters talking together.

Choose *two* of the combinations below:
   officer/owner
   officer/accused pupil
   owner/parent of accused pupil
   schoolfriend/reporter
   owner/reporter

customer/reporter
schoolfriend/teacher
accused pupil/older brother or sister
schoolfriend/officer

 Work on each of your choices in turn — first as a spoken activity, then writing them as playscripts.

Don't forget to include the information and directions for readers and actors.

Extra ideas

 1. Make up your own incident outline (as brief as the café one), and either script the whole scene, or a dialogue between two of the characters involved in it.
2. Write the dialogue between two neighbours the morning after one of them held a very noisy party.
3. Write the dialogue of the confrontation between a store detective and a person suspected of shoplifting.
4. Script a scene in which the interest lies in the way one person keeps interrupting the other.

A Night Out

The following extract is the opening scene from Harold Pinter's play *A Night Out*. It consists of a dialogue between Albert and his mother.

A Night Out

by HAROLD PINTER

The kitchen of MRS STOKES' *small house in the south of London. Clean and tidy.*

ALBERT, *a young man of twenty-eight, is standing in his shirt and trousers, combing his hair in the kitchen mirror over the mantelpiece. A woman's voice calls his name from upstairs. He ignores it, picks up a brush from the mantelpiece and brushes his hair. The voice calls again. He slips the comb in his pocket, bends down, reaches under the sink and takes out a shoe duster. He begins to polish his shoes.* MRS STOKES *descends the stairs, passes through the hall and enters the kitchen.*

MOTHER: Albert, I've been calling you. (*She watches him.*)
    What are you doing?
ALBERT: Nothing.

45

MOTHER: Didn't you hear me call you, Albert? I've been calling you from upstairs.

ALBERT: You seen my tie?

MOTHER: Oh, I say, I'll have to put the flag out.

ALBERT: What do you mean?

MOTHER: Cleaning your shoes, Albert? I'll have to put the flag out, won't I?

ALBERT *puts the brush back under the sink and begins to search the sideboard and cupboard.*

What are you looking for?

ALBERT: My tie. The striped one, the blue one.

MOTHER: The bulb's gone in Grandma's room.

ALBERT: Has it?

MOTHER: That's what I was calling you about. I went in and switched on the light and the bulb had gone.

She watches him open the kitchen cabinet and look into it.

Aren't those your best trousers, Albert? What have you put on your best trousers for?

ALBERT: Look, Mum, where's my tie? The blue one, the blue tie, where is it? You know the one I mean, the blue striped one, I gave it to you this morning.

MOTHER: What do you want your tie for?

ALBERT: I want to put it on. I asked you to press it for me this morning. I gave it to you this morning before I went to work, didn't I?

She goes to the gas stove, examines the vegetables, opens the oven and looks into it.

MOTHER (*gently*): Well, your dinner'll be ready soon. You can look for it afterwards. Lay the table, there's a good boy.

ALBERT: Why should I look for it afterwards? You know where it is now.

MOTHER: You've got five minutes. Go down to the cellar, Albert, get a bulb and put it in Grandma's room, go on.

ALBERT (*irritably*): I don't know why you keep calling that room Grandma's room, she's been dead ten years.

MOTHER: Albert!

ALBERT: I mean, it's just a junk room, that's all it is.

MOTHER: Albert, that's no way to speak about your Grandma, you know that as well as I do.

ALBERT: I'm not saying a word against Grandma —

MOTHER: You'll upset me in a minute, you go on like that.

ALBERT: I'm not going on about anything.

MOTHER: Yes, you are. Now why don't you go and put a bulb in Grandma's room and by the time you come down I'll have your dinner on the table.

ALBERT: I can't go down to the cellar, I've got my best trousers on, I've got a white shirt on.

MOTHER: You're dressing up tonight, aren't you? Dressing up, cleaning your shoes, anyone would think you were going to the Ritz.

ALBERT: I'm not going to the Ritz.

MOTHER (*suspiciously*): What do you mean, you're not going to the Ritz?

ALBERT: What do you mean?

MOTHER: The way you said you're not going to the Ritz, it sounded like you were going somewhere else.

ALBERT (*wearily*): I am.

MOTHER (*shocked surprise*): You're going out?

ALBERT: You know I'm going out. I told you I was going out. I told you last week. I told you this morning. Look, where's my tie? I've got to have my tie. I'm late already. Come on, Mum, where'd you put it?

MOTHER: What about your dinner?

ALBERT (*searching*): Look . . . I told you . . . I haven't got the . . . wait a minute . . . ah, here it is.

MOTHER: You can't wear that tie. I haven't pressed it.

ALBERT: You have. Look at it. Of course you have. It's beautifully pressed. It's fine.

He ties the tie.

MOTHER: Where are you going?

ALBERT: Mum, I've told you, honestly, three times. Honestly, I've told you three times I had to go out tonight.

MOTHER: No, you didn't.

ALBERT *exclaims and knots the tie.*

I thought you were joking.

ALBERT: I'm not going . . . I'm just going to Mr King's. I've told you. You don't believe me.

MOTHER: You're going to Mr King's?

ALBERT: Mr Ryan's leaving. You know Ryan. He's leaving the firm. He's been there years. So Mr King's giving a sort of party for him at his house . . . well, not exactly a party, not a party, just a few . . . you know . . . anyway, we're all invited. I've got to go. Everyone else is going. I've got to go. I don't want to go, but I've got to.

MOTHER (*bewildered, sitting*): Well, I don't know . . .

ALBERT (*with his arm round her*): I won't be late. I don't want to go. I'd much rather stay with you.

MOTHER: Would you?

ALBERT: You know I would. Who wants to go to Mr King's party?

MOTHER: We were going to have our game of cards.

ALBERT: Well, we can't have our game of cards.
(*Pause.*)

MOTHER: Put the bulb in Grandma's room, Albert.

ALBERT: I've told you I'm not going down to the cellar in my white shirt. There's no light in the cellar either. I'll be pitch black in five minutes, looking for those bulbs.

MOTHER: I told you to put a light in the cellar. I told you yesterday.

ALBERT: Well, I can't do it now.

MOTHER: If we had a light in the cellar you'd be able to see where those bulbs were. You don't expect me to go down to the cellar?

ALBERT: I don't know why we keep bulbs in the cellar!
(*Pause.*)

MOTHER: Your father would turn in his grave if he heard you raise your voice to me. You're all I've got, Albert. I want you to remember that. I haven't got anyone else. I want you . . . I want you to bear that in mind.

ALBERT: I'm sorry . . . I raised my voice.

He goes to the door.

(*Mumbling.*) I've got to go.

MOTHER (*following*): Albert!

ALBERT: What?

MOTHER: I want to ask you a question.

ALBERT: What?

MOTHER: Are you leading a clean life?

ALBERT: A clean life?

MOTHER: You're not leading an unclean life, are you?

ALBERT: What are you talking about?

MOTHER: You're not messing about with girls, are you?
   You're not going to go messing about with girls tonight?

ALBERT: Don't be so ridiculous.

MOTHER: Answer me, Albert. I'm your mother.

ALBERT: I don't know any girls.

MOTHER: If you're going to the firm's party, there'll be girls
   there, won't there? Girls from the office?

ALBERT: I don't like them, any of them.

MOTHER: You promise?

ALBERT: Promise what?

MOTHER: That . . . that you won't upset your father.

ALBERT: My father? How can I upset my father? You're
   always talking about upsetting people who are dead!

MOTHER: Oh, Albert, you don't know how you hurt me, you
   don't know the hurtful way you've got, speaking of your
   poor father like that.

ALBERT: But he is dead.

MOTHER: He's not! He's living! (*Touching her breast.*) In here!
   And this is his house!
   (*Pause.*)

ALBERT: Look, Mum, I won't be late . . . and I won't . . .

MOTHER: But what about your dinner? It's nearly ready.

ALBERT: Seeley and Kedge are waiting for me. I told you not
   to cook dinner this morning. (*He goes to the stairs.*) Just
   because you never listen . . .

*He runs up the stairs and disappears. She calls after him
from the hall.*

MOTHER: Well, what am I going to do while you're out? I
   can't go into Grandma's room because there's no light. I
   can't go down to the cellar in the dark, we were going to
   have a game of cards, it's Friday night, what about our game
   of rummy?

HAROLD PINTER

49

Looking back

1. Discuss in a group:
   ▶ What are the tactics used by Albert's mother to prevent him from going out?
   ▶ Where in the script are two or three moments when Albert comes close to losing his temper? How do you know?

2. Prepare a radio performance of part or the whole of this scene. You could take the roles of two actors, a script adviser/director, and a sound-effects person.
   ▶ How are you going to deal with the stage directions and sounds? Are all of them needed for radio?
   ▶ This could be tape recorded or given a live performance.

3. Prepare a group improvisation in which one or both parents try to prevent a young person going out for the evening. Emphasise the tactics that might be used. (This could be scripted afterwards.)

Extra ideas

All these ideas could be discussed or improvised before being written.

1. Write a monologue for Albert's mother to last for about three minutes after he leaves.

2. Imagine Albert meets Seeley or Kedge (or possibly a girl) in the pub round the corner from his home. Write a dialogue for them in which Albert explains why he is late and in which they discuss what they are *really* going to do for the evening.

3. Albert arrives home at 3.00 a.m. His mother is still waiting up for him. Write the dialogue which takes place — being careful to keep close to Pinter's original characters.

4. What's your opinion of this opening scene? What do you think of the way in which Pinter has presented
   ▶ the characters
   ▶ the relationship between them
   ▶ the way they speak
   ▶ the situation?

   Has he managed to provide the readers/audience with an interesting start? Is it humorous? Tense? Intriguing?

5

BRIEF LIVES

WORKING ON SHORT STORIES

This section contains three short stories, and three very short stories. Whether they are read aloud in class, or silently to yourself, you should discuss each story in a pair or group, before, during and after reading. This is intended to help you understand and enjoy the story and be better prepared to write about it.

Each of the three stories that follow is of a different type, or genre. One is a science fiction story, another a romance, and another a mystery.

Looking ahead

Before reading 'Who's There?', look closely at the title and the first paragraph.

Who's There?

When Satellite Control called me, I was writing up the day's progress report in the Observation Bubble — the glass-domed office that juts out from the axis of the Space Station like the hubcap of a wheel. It was not really a good place to work, for the view was too overwhelming. Only a few yards away I could see the construction teams performing their slow-motion ballet as they put the station together like a giant jigsaw puzzle. And beyond them, twenty thousand miles below, was the blue-green glory of the full Earth, floating against the ravelled star clouds of the Milky Way.

Discuss these questions and record your responses:
▶ What type of story is it?
▶ Where is the story set?
▶ Is it past, present or future time?
▶ Is the narrator (the 'I' in the story) a man or woman?
▶ Does he/she have an important job?
▶ Consider the title again. What could the story be about?

'Station Supervisor here,' I answered. 'What's the trouble?'
'Our radar's showing a small echo two miles away, almost stationary, about five degrees west of Sirius. Can you give us a visual report on it?'

Anything matching our orbit so precisely could hardly be a meteor; it would have to be something we'd dropped — perhaps an inadequately secured piece of equipment that had drifted away from the station. So I assumed; but when I pulled out my binoculars and searched the sky around Orion, I soon found my mistake. Though this space traveller was man-made, it had nothing to do with us.

'I've found it,' I told Control. 'It's someone's test satellite — cone-shaped, four antennae, and what looks like a lens system in its base. Probably U.S. Air Force, early nineteen-sixties, judging by the design. I know they lost track of several when their transmitters failed. There were quite a few attempts to hit this orbit before they finally made it.'

After a brief search through the files Control was able to confirm my guess. It took a little longer to find out that Washington wasn't in the least bit interested in our discovery of a twenty-year-old stray satellite, and would be just as happy if we lost it again.

'Well, we can't do *that*,' said Control. 'Even if nobody wants it, the thing's a menace to navigation. Someone had better go out and haul it aboard.'

That someone, I realized, would have to be me. I dared not detach a man from the closely knit construction teams, for we were already behind schedule — and a single day's delay on this job cost a million dollars. All the radio and TV networks on Earth were waiting impatiently for the moment when they could route their programmes through us, and thus provide the first truly global service, spanning the world from Pole to Pole.

'I'll go out and get it,' I answered, snapping an elastic band over my papers so that the air currents from the ventilators wouldn't set them wandering around the room. Though I tried to sound as if I was doing everyone a great favour, I was secretly not at all displeased. It had been at least two weeks since I'd been outside; I was getting a little tired of stores schedules, maintenance reports, and all the glamorous ingredients of a Space Station Supervisor's life.

The only member of the staff I passed on my way to the air lock was Tommy, our recently acquired cat. Pets mean a great deal to men thousands of miles from Earth, but there are not many animals that can adapt themselves to a weightless environment. Tommy mewed plaintively at me as I clambered into my spacesuit, but I was in too much of a hurry to play with him.

At this point, perhaps I should remind you that the suits we use on the station are completely different from the flexible affairs men wear when they want to walk around on the moon. Ours are really baby spaceships, just big enough to hold one man. They are stubby cylinders, about seven feet long, fitted with low-powered propulsion jets, and have a pair of accordion-like sleeves at the upper end for the operator's arms. Normally, however, you keep your hands drawn inside the suit, working the manual controls in front of your chest.

As soon as I'd settled down inside my very exclusive spacecraft, I switched on power and checked the gauges on the tiny instrument panel. There's a magic word, 'FORB', that you'll often hear spacemen mutter as they climb into their suits; it reminds them to test fuel, oxygen, radio, batteries. All my needles were well in the safety zone, so I lowered the transparent hemisphere over my head and sealed myself in. For a short trip like this I did not bother to check the suit's internal lockers, which were used to carry food and special equipment for extended missions.

As the conveyor belt decanted me into the air lock I felt like an Indian papoose being carried along on its mother's back. Then the pumps brought the pressure down to zero, the outer door opened, and the last traces of air swept me out into the stars, turning very slowly head over heels.

The station was only a dozen feet away, yet I was now an independent planet — a little world of my own. I was sealed up in a tiny, mobile cylinder, with a superb view of the entire universe, but I had practically no freedom of movement inside the suit. The padded seat and safety belts prevented me from turning around, though I could reach all the controls and lockers with my hands or feet.

In space, the great enemy is the sun, which can blast you to blindness in seconds. Very cautiously, I opened up the dark filters on the 'night' side of my suit, and turned my head to look out at the stars. At the same time I switched the helmet's external sunshade to automatic, so that whichever way the suit gyrated my eyes would be shielded from that intolerable glare.

Presently, I found my target — a bright fleck of silver whose metallic glint distinguished it clearly from the surrounding stars. I stamped on the jet-control pedal, and felt the mild surge of acceleration as the low-powered rockets set me moving away from the station. After ten seconds of steady thrust I estimated that my speed was great enough, and cut off the drive. It would take me five minutes to coast the rest of the way, and not much longer to return with my salvage.

And it was at that moment, as I launched myself out into the abyss, that I knew that something was horribly wrong.

▶ How do you think the story will develop?

It is never completely silent inside a spacesuit; you can always hear the gentle hiss of oxygen, the faint whirr of fans and motors, the susurration of your own breathing — even, if you listen carefully enough, the rhythmic thump that is the pounding of your heart. These sounds reverberate through the suit, unable to escape into the surrounding void; they are the unnoticed background of life in space, for you are aware of them only when they change.

They had changed now; to them had been added a sound which I could not identify. It was an intermittent, muffled thudding, sometimes accompanied by a scraping noise, as of metal upon metal.

I froze instantly, holding my breath and trying to locate the alien sound with my ears. The meters on the control board gave no clues; all the needles were rock-steady on their scales, and there were none of the flickering red lights that would warn of impending disaster. That was some comfort, but not much. I had long ago learned to trust my instincts in such matters; their alarm signals were flashing now, telling me to return to the station before it was too late. . . .

Even now, I do not like to recall those next few minutes, as panic slowly flooded into my mind like a rising tide, overwhelming the dams of reason and logic which every man must erect against the mystery of the universe. I knew then what it was like to face insanity: no other explanation fitted the facts.

For it was no longer possible to pretend that the noise disturbing me was that of some faulty mechanism. Though I was in utter isolation, far from any other human being or indeed any material object, I was not alone. The soundless void was bringing to my ears the faint but unmistakable stirrings of life.

In that first, heart-freezing moment it seemed that something was trying to get into my suit — something invisible, seeking shelter from the cruel and pitiless vacuum of space. I whirled madly in my harness, scanning the entire sphere of vision around me except for the blazing, forbidden cone toward the sun. There was nothing there, of course. There could not be — yet that purposeful scrabbling was clearer than ever.

Despite the nonsense that has been written about us, it is not true that spacemen are superstitious. But can you blame me if, as I came to the end of logic's resources, I suddenly remembered how Bernie Summers had died, no farther from the station than I was at this very moment?

It was one of those 'impossible' accidents; it always is. Three things had gone wrong at once. Bernie's oxygen regulator had run wild and sent the pressure soaring, the safety valve had failed to blow — and a faulty joint had given way instead. In a fraction of a second, his suit was open to space.

I had never known Bernie, but suddenly his fate became of overwhelming importance to me — for a horrible idea had come into my mind. One does not talk about these things, but a damaged spacesuit is too valuable to be thrown away, even if it has killed its wearer. It is repaired, renumbered — and issued to someone else. . . .

What happens to the soul of a man who dies between the stars, far from his native world? Are you still here, Bernie, clinging to the last object that linked you to your lost and distant home?

As I fought the nightmares that were swirling around me — for now it seemed that the scratchings and soft fumblings were coming from all directions — there was one last hope to which I clung. For the sake of my sanity I had to prove that this wasn't Bernie's suit — that the metal walls so closely wrapped around me had never been another man's coffin.

It took me several tries before I could press the right button and switch my transmitter to the emergency wave length. 'Station!' I gasped. 'I'm in trouble! Get records to check my suit history and —'

I never finished; they say my yell wrecked the microphone. But what man alone in the absolute isolation of a spacesuit would *not* have yelled when something patted him softly on the back of the neck?

I must have lunged forward, despite the safety harness, and smashed against the upper edge of the control panel. When the rescue squad reached me a few minutes later, I was still unconscious, with an angry bruise across my forehead.

And so I was the last person in the whole satellite relay system to know what had happened. When I came to my senses an hour later all our medical staff were gathered around my bed, but it was quite a while before the doctors bothered to look at me. They were much too busy playing with the three cute little kittens our badly misnamed Tommy had been rearing in the seclusion of my spacesuit's Number Five Storage Locker.

A. C. Clarke

Looking back

Did the ending
▶ surprise you
▶ disappoint you
▶ seem believable
▶ make you laugh?

How does the writer build up the tension towards the end? Is it
▶ the use of certain words
▶ the length of sentence
▶ the pace of the story
▶ the fact that we are 'inside' the head of the narrator, living his experiences?

What do you think is the main theme of the story? Is it
▶ the marvels of technology
▶ the fun of pets
▶ the irony of human error
▶ the limits of logic
▶ the possibility of life after death
▶ life's a funny old game
or something else?

For writing

1. Write a story set in the future, in which some apparent mystery has a quite simple solution.
2. Imagine the narrator goes back to the Observation Bubble to write up the day's progress report. What would that report have to say about the day's events?

SPACE STATION ZX40
DATE: 6.4.2047
PLACE: SIRIUS
REPORT FROM : STATION SUPERVISOR
            TO: SATELLITE CONTROL

3. Use the notes you have taken to compare your predictions of the story and the actual story. Whose version do you prefer?

Looking ahead

Read the first paragraph of 'The Kiss' and then discuss the questions and record your responses.

The Kiss

I'd idolized Bill Taylor for months. It was a secret and undeclared passion and began in a ballroom dancing class in the old church hall.

▶ What type of story is this?
▶ Is it set in the past, present or future?
▶ What sort of person is the narrator (the 'I' in this story)?
▶ What do you think this story will be about?

I saw him, leaning against the window frame, smoking, laughing with the other boys. He had blue eyes and curly fair hair which he had dampened and brushed back in the manner of the day so the curls rippled over his head like waves.

He didn't choose me to be his partner of course, and my friend Anne and I ended up together again and arguing as to who was going to be the man. Once I brushed against him as I was being pushed blind into a complicated spin-turn by Anne. He apologised and so did I. He had a green cord jacket on.

He never came to another class but each week was exciting just anticipating him being there and the disappointment died as the hope for the next week was born.

Then — there was to be a dance in St Aloysius Hall, tickets in aid of the new Scout den. It was arranged by the local Rover group and Bill Taylor was a Rover. He'd be bound to be there.

I put on my best blue check dress with the velvet covered buttons and trim round the collar, and borrowed my sister's blue sheer stockings with seams, though my suspender belt cut deeply and painfully into my hips. I also borrowed her make-up and drew little smudgy grey lines on my eyelids and mascara'd my eyelashes until my eyes watered.

The dance followed the usual pattern. For the first hour we, the girls, stood in the hall, trembling with excitement, at one end, with all the boys at

the other and a few mums and dads or elder brothers and sisters dancing in the space between.

Boredom, then depression followed on. The evening was nearly over and Anne and I had only danced with each other and there'd been no sign of Bill Taylor. She stared gloomily one way and I the other, watching the couples twirl and spin.

'Do you want a coke?' she asked me.

'Yeh — all this dancing makes you so hot.'

'Don't be like that.'

There we stood sipping coke through straws, wallflowers in first bloom. Anne nudged me — she saw him first. Bill Taylor was edging his way round the rim of the dance floor. He appeared to be searching for someone — but not for us, for he looked right over our heads.

Then he must have suddenly realised he was looking through someone he knew:

'Hello.'

'Hello,' I gulped.

'I've just arrived. I was looking for the others,' he said vaguely, still peering into the half light.

He must have realized it was a hopeless task. He shrugged his shoulders.

'Ah well — how's it going?'

'Fine,' I lied.

A pause. 'Would you like a dance?'

I couldn't believe it! But what about Anne? I gave her a questioning look.

'Will you be OK?'

'Go on!' She gave me a shove.

'Oh — hang on,' I called to Bill. 'My coke!' I explained.

I sucked vigorously and gulped the bubbles down — pushed the tin into Anne's hand and turned after him.

It was a jerky number, loud and tuneless and we'd just got into a kind of rhythmic waggle when the music stopped and we stood awkwardly facing each other, waiting for the music to start again.

It was a slow smooch, I realized, with a mixture of delight and horror. He looked at me for a split second and then, resigning himself to his fate, he put his arm lightly round my waist, his green cord jacket brushed against my cheek and I was in seventh heaven, his hand damp on my waist, the smell of the smoke on his breath, the music romantic, coiling its sound round us.

Then it happened, rather suddenly, and there was nothing I could do. I felt the bubbles of coke rising inside me. If I opened my mouth an enormous burp would emerge so I kept my mouth shut and tried to divert the air through my nose. There was an extraordinary sensation at the back of my throat and then a fine cascade of silver froth burst from my nostrils and tumbled down the front of Bill's green cord jacket.

'What's the matter!' he sprang away. I think he thought I was being sick.

'I'm so sorry — it was the coke — it came down my nose.' I wiped ineffectually at his coat with my hand. Fortunately he laughed — and so did I and he wiped the lapel with a handkerchief but the music had finished and the spell had been broken. He saw his friends over the other side of the room and with a polite 'Thanks — excuse me — I've just seen the others,' he was gone.

I don't think I saw him again for weeks after that episode. It was my friend and dancing partner Anne who brought about the next development.

'My parents have said I can have a party on my birthday. Three weeks time, since it falls on a Saturday this year.'

'Oh great! you can ask Bill!'

'Hang on! Hang on! First things first! Anyway how can we ask him? We don't know where he lives.'

There were lots of preparations to fill the days; ordering drink, borrowing glasses from the pub, and the invitations to pass around. But the problem of how to invite Bill obsessed me. Finally Anne's brother Ed was enlisted to help. He knew Lawrence, who was Bill's best mate, and he'd tell them both. We couldn't be sure he'd come — but on the morning of the party Eddie swore for the tenth time that the message had been delivered.

The afternoon was taken up with the terrible labour of moving furniture, rolling carpets, putting vases and photos and breakables away, sprinkling ashtrays in the shape of saucers and shells, liberally around the front and back rooms. Eddie was in charge of records — music would be in the back room and we'd leave the heavy furniture in the front room for those who wanted to sit around and talk. Together we pushed the deep old-fashioned armchairs and settees back to the corners of the room and sprinkled the cushions over the rest of the floor.

I barely had time to bath and pull the blue check dress on again, wishing I had something else I could wear instead but there was no time to dwell on it. The blue stockings were sneaked out of my sister's drawer again and this time I picked up a blue pearly Alice band from her dressing table and brushed my hair loose and back behind my ears, pinning it neatly with this band.

By the time I arrived Anne was already in despair, crying her eyes out in her bedroom whilst a few guests clung to the walls and ate crisps downstairs.

'What's the matter? Anne? For goodness sake! Speak to me.'

'It's a failure — nobody's going to come! I hate parties anyway.'

'Don't be silly — there are lots of people here already. Things are always slow at the beginning, now come on!'

I wetted a flannel under the tap and patted her swollen eyes. I slipped her into her dress and brushed her hair for her till it shone.

'I look awful,' she wailed.

'Nonsense — anyway there aren't many lights on and no-one will see.'

Down we went together, I secretly feeling no more confident than she.

But people were indeed arriving and Ed had an LP of Elvis Presley shaking the room. The kitchen was soon awash in beer and cider and the hallway blocked with people struggling to and fro holding paper cups aloft.

Anne and I stood at the bottom of the stairs by the telephone.

'Do you know all these people?' I asked her.

'No,' she looked glum.

Then her face brightened suddenly as a gangly youth in a red crash helmet strode through the door.

'He's come!' she cried.

'Who? Bill?'

'No — silly!'

And she darted off and up to him, taking his helmet to safety, the gracious hostess and birthday girl.

I recognized a couple of Anne's school mates and chatted to them before they slid away into the kitchen. I was about to follow when the door swung open again and this time it was Bill. My heart beat heavily and I felt myself colour. He looked round vacantly and then saw me.

'Hello again.'

'Hello.'

'I've come to the right place then.'

'Yes.'

'Where shall I put this?' He held a party beer can up.

'Follow the mass!'

'Right!'

And off he went leaving me to think of all the witty, arresting things I could have said:

'I'll take it through! Ah good, drink's arrived — I've been waiting for something good to walk through that door. Let's open it here.'

I couldn't follow him now — it would be too obvious. I'd have to walk into the front room and pretend I was going there anyway. There were couples spread-eagled on the cushions, on the floor — wound together on the settee. Only the big armchair was unoccupied — I turned back and wandered into the dancing room. Eddie was standing by the record player watching the couples dancing where the dining room table usually stood.

'Having a good time?' he asked as I looked through the pile of records.

'Yes — in a way.'

'Has he come then?'

'Who?' I flushed.

'Your Rover Scout.'

'I don't know.' I moved off again, into the kitchen for a glass of something. Empty bottles covered the sideboard and the kitchen table and I picked up each in turn.

'Here's some cider — do you like cider?' asked a strange man with little round glasses and a pale blue tee-shirt.

'If there's nothing else — thanks!'

He laughed — 'Yes — I'm like that too. Stick to beer as long as it lasts and then as a last resort onto the cider — dry first — last of all, the sweet! Mind you — I'd go for the wine too, if it was around — wouldn't say no to a drop of the white. I prefer white to red myself. Got terribly drunk on the red once — mind you' — I shifted from one foot to the other trying to maintain interest — 'not as bad as sherry — worst hangover ever I got from sherry. Can't touch it now. Even the smell — you know — sort of brings it all back.' He laughed at his own wit. I smiled and moved as if to go.

'Do you want to dance?' he asked eagerly.

'Well — er — I'm a bit hot actually!'

'Oh.' His face dropped for an instant.

'Well — it does make you sweat a bit, does dancing — anyway — you can't really talk — all this loud music — can't stand this one — whatever it is.'

'It's Elvis!' I said hotly.

'Oh — you like it do you — no accounting for taste.'

There was a pause and I seized my opportunity.

'Excuse me — I've got to go and join the queue!'

'Queue?' he looked blank.

'Bathroom.'

'Oh I see — yes sure — I'll wait here.'

Wait, would he! He'd have to wait a long time. I slipped out and back to my spot by the telephone.

'Come on,' said a voice and I was gripped by the hand at the same time. I whirled round — it was Bill.

He led me to the front room, to the big armchair. He sat down and patted his knee, and I sat woodenly, like a ventriloquist's dummy. I don't think we said anything.

He settled back and I rested my head on that green cord jacket. I hardly dared breathe lest I should break the spell.

His hand was rubbing up and down my back gently. I almost fell asleep it was so soothing.

Then I felt him shifting and I lifted my head an inch or two — he was staring at me. I thought I should say something and was just about to when his lips closed on mine in my first kiss. He pushed hard and I could feel his teeth break the skin.

My pulse was beating. He was pulling my head down — suddenly I felt something had hit my nose — my pearly Alice band. My eyelashes caught against it — perhaps Bill's did too for he broke away and I was left panting with a blue Alice band across my eyes. He pulled it off and dropped it behind him onto the floor and with barely enough time to draw breath he pulled my mouth towards his — his lips forced mine open and our teeth chipped painfully.

So we kissed the night away, pausing only to surface for air and to pull wisps of my hair from our mouths whilst Elvis and Adam and Mick strummed their guitars.

Then it was all over. We were struggling up and lights were turned on. I stood blinking like an owl in the middle of the room while Bill lit a cigarette. Anne came scurrying in emptying ashtrays, collecting glasses and bottles.

'I'd better help,' I said to Bill.

'Yes — sure — I must go — so long.'

And that was that.

All that night I kept waking, gasping for breath, with his lips on mine and my heart thumping and next day I woke with a headache and a bruised chin. I saw him that very day coming towards me along the road. It was me who turned, cheeks hot, pulse beating and I walked quickly, obviously away from him.

I still don't know why.

Christine Purkis

Looking back

The story is obviously set in the past. What elements in the story would be different for a romance written today? Would it be the language, the fashions, the attitudes, or what? Make a list of those things that convinced you the story was set in the past.

▶ Do girls and boys inevitably act differently in these situations? Here is a list of comments made in the story:

'I've just arrived. I was looking for the others.'

'Would you like a dance?'

'I'm so sorry — it was the coke — it came down my nose.'

'I hate parties anyway.'

'I prefer white to red myself. Got terribly drunk on the red once — mind you.'

'Well — er — I'm a bit hot actually!'

'Excuse me — I've got to go and join the queue!'

▶ Who said them in the story? Could they have been spoken by a girl or a boy equally easily?

▶ What conclusions could you draw from your answers?

▶ Why does the narrator walk away from Bill at the end? Would any other ending have suited the story better, in your opinion?

Extra ideas

Write an alternative ending to the story. You could begin with the sentence: 'I saw him that very day coming towards me along the road.' Try to keep to the same style as the original.

The story is written from one character's point of view. What do you think Bill's attitude is? Write the story from his point of view.

Many magazines today have 'advice columns' which contain suggestions for coping with various personal problems. Construct the letter that the narrator might have written about her courtship difficulties and then offer your advice. You could read some actual advice comments first to get to grips with a suitable style.

Looking ahead

The Emissary

Martin knew it was autumn again, for Dog ran into the house bringing wind and frost and a smell of apples turned to cider under trees. In dark clock-springs of hair, Dog fetched goldenrod, dust of farewell-summer, acorn-husk, hair of squirrel, feather of departed robin, sawdust from fresh-cut cordwood, and leaves like charcoals shaken from a blaze of maple trees. Dog jumped. Showers of brittle fern, blackberry vine, marsh-grass sprang over the bed where Martin shouted. No doubt, no doubt of it at all, this incredible beast was October!

'Here, boy, here!'

And Dog settled to warm Martin's body with all the bonfires and subtle burnings of the season, to fill the room with soft or heavy, wet or dry odours of far-travelling. In spring, he smelled of lilac, iris, lawn-mowed grass; in summer, ice-cream moustached, he came pungent with firecracker, Roman candle, pinwheel, baked by the sun. But Autumn! Autumn!

'Dog, what's it like outside?'

And lying there, Dog told as he always told. Lying there, Martin found autumn as in the old days before sickness bleached him white on his bed. Here was his contact, his carry-all, the quick-moving part of himself he sent with a yell to run and return, circle and scent, collect and deliver the time and texture of worlds in town, country, by creek, river, lake, down-cellar, up-attic, in closet or coal-bin. Ten dozen times a day he was gifted with sunflower seed, cinder-path, milkweed, horse-chestnut, or full flame-smell of pumpkin. Through the loomings of the universe Dog shuttled; the design was his in his pelt. Put out your hand, it was there. . . .

'And where did you go this morning?'

But he knew without hearing where Dog had rattled down hills where autumn lay in cereal crispness, where children lay in funeral pyres, in rustling heaps, the leaf-buried but watchful dead, as Dog and the world blew by. Martin trembled his fingers, searched the thick fur, read the long journey. Through stubbled fields, over glitters of ravine creek, down marbled spread of cemetery yard, into woods. In the great season of spices and rare incense, now Martin ran through his emissary, around, about, and home!

An emissary is a messenger, or agent, and its associations are often with secret or difficult missions. Do the opening few paragraphs seem to support such an interpretation or not?

Now read on.

The bedroom door opened.

'That dog of yours is in trouble again.'

Mother brought in a tray of fruit salad, cocoa, and toast, her blue eyes snapping.

'Mother . . .'

'Always digging places. Dug a hole in Miss Tarkin's garden this morning. She's spittin' mad. That's the fourth hole he's dug there this week.'

'Maybe he's looking for something.'

'Fiddlesticks, he's too darned curious. If he doesn't behave he'll be locked up.'

Martin looked at this woman as if she were a stranger.

'Oh, you wouldn't do that! How would I learn anything? How would I find things out if Dog didn't tell me?'

Mom's voice was quieter. 'Is that what he does — tell you things?'

'There's nothing I don't know when he goes out and around and back, *nothing* I can't find out from him!'

They both sat looking at Dog and the dry strewings of mould and seed over the quilt.

'Well, if he'll just stop digging where he shouldn't, he can run all he wants,' said Mother.

'Here, boy, here!'

And Martin snapped a tin note to the dog's collar:

MY OWNER IS MARTIN SMITH — TEN YEARS OLD — SICK IN BED — VISITORS WELCOME.

Dog barked. Mother opened the downstairs door and let him out.

Martin sat listening.

Far off and away you could hear Dog in the quiet autumn rain that was
falling now. You could hear the barking-jingling fade, rise, fade again as he
cut down alley, over lawn, to fetch back Mr Holloway and the oiled metallic
smell of the delicate snowflake-interiored watches he repaired in his home
shop. Or maybe he would bring Mr Jacobs, the grocer, whose clothes were
rich with lettuce, celery, tomatoes, and the secret tinned and hidden smell
of the red demons stamped on cans of devilled ham. Mr Jacobs and his
unseen pink-meat devils waved often from the yard below. Or Dog brought
Mr Jackson, Mrs Gillespie, Mr Smith, Mrs Holmes, *any* friend or near-
friend, encountered, cornered, begged, worried, and at last shepherded
home for lunch, or tea-and-biscuits.

Now, listening, Martin heard Dog below, with footsteps moving in a light
rain behind him. The downstairs bell rang, Mom opened the door, light
voices murmured. Martin sat forward, face shining. The stair treads
creaked. A young woman's voice laughed quietly. Miss Haight, of course,
his teacher from school!

The bedroom door sprang open.

Martin had company.

▶ Why is Martin confined to his room?

▶ Is Dog's behaviour creditable?

▶ What is the effect of the narrator also being confined to Martin's
room?

▶ Can you predict what is going to happen in the story?

Morning, afternoon, evening, dawn and dusk, sun and moon circled with
Dog, who faithfully reported temperatures of turf and air, colour of earth
and tree, consistency of mist or rain, but — most important of all —
brought back again and again — Miss Haight.

On Saturday, Sunday and Monday she baked Martin orange-iced
cupcakes, brought him library books about dinosaurs and cavemen. On
Tuesday, Wednesday and Thursday somehow he beat her at dominoes,
somehow she lost at checkers, and soon, she cried, he'd defeat her
handsomely at chess. On Friday, Saturday and Sunday they talked and
never stopped talking, and she was so young and laughing and handsome
and her hair was a soft, shining brown like the season outside the window,
and she walked clear, clean and quick, a heartbeat warm in the bitter
afternoon when he heard it. Above all, she had the secret of signs, and
could read and interpret Dog and the symbols she searched out and
plucked forth from his coat with her miraculous fingers. Eyes shut, softly
laughing, in a gypsy's voice, she divined the world from the treasures in her
hands.

And on Monday afternoon, Miss Haight was dead.

Martin sat up in bed, slowly.

'Dead?' he whispered.

Dead, said his mother, yes, dead, killed in an auto accident a mile out of town. Dead, yes, dead, which meant cold to Martin, which meant silence and whiteness and winter come long before its time. Dead, silent, cold, white. The thoughts circled round, blew down, and settled in whispers.

Martin held Dog, thinking; turned to the wall. The lady with the autumn-coloured hair. The lady with the laughter that was very gentle and never made fun and the eyes that watched your mouth to see everything you ever said. The-other-half-of-autumn-lady, who told what was left untold by Dog, about the world. The heartbeat at the still centre of grey afternoon. The heartbeat fading . . .

'Mom? What do they do in the graveyard, Mom, under the ground? Just lay there?'

'*Lie* there.'

'Lie there? Is that *all* they do? It doesn't sound like much fun.'

'For goodness sake, it's not made out to be fun.'

'Why don't they jump up and run around once in a while if they get tired lying there? God's pretty silly —'

'Martin!'

'Well, you'd think He'd treat people better than to tell them to lie still for keeps. That's impossible. Nobody can do it! I tried once. Dog tries. I tell him, "dead Dog!" He plays dead awhile, then gets sick and tired and wags his tail or opens one eye and looks at me, bored. Boy, I bet sometimes those graveyard people do the same, huh, Dog?'

Dog barked.

'Be still with that kind of talk!' said Mother.

Martin looked off into space.

'Bet that's exactly what they do,' he said.

Autumn burnt the trees bare and ran Dog still farther around, fording creek, prowling graveyard as was his custom, and back in the dusk to fire off volleys of barking that shook windows wherever he turned.

In the late last days of October, Dog began to act as if the wind had changed and blew from a strange country. He stood quivering on the porch below. He whined, his eyes fixed at the empty land beyond town. He brought no visitors for Martin. He stood for hours each day, as if leashed, trembling, then shot away straight, as if someone had called. Each night, he returned later, with no one following. Each night, Martin sank deeper and deeper in his pillow.

'Well, people are busy,' said Mother. 'They haven't time to notice the tag Dog carries. Or they mean to come visit, but forget.'

But there was more to it than that. There was the fevered shining in Dog's eyes, and his whimpering tic late at night, in some private dream. His shivering in the dark, under the bed. The way he sometimes stood half the night, looking at Martin as if some great and impossible secret was his and he knew no way to tell it save by savagely thumping his tail, or turning in endless circles, never to lie down, spinning and spinning again.

On October thirtieth, Dog ran out and didn't come back at all, even when after supper Martin heard his parents call and call. The hour grew late, the streets and sidewalks stood empty, the air moved cold about the house and there was nothing, nothing.

Long after midnight, Martin lay watching the world beyond the cool, clear glass windows. Now there was not even autumn, for there was no Dog to fetch it in. There would be no winter, for who could bring the snow to melt in your hands? Father, Mother? No, not the same. They couldn't play the game with its special secrets and rules, its sounds and panto-mimes. No more seasons. No more time. The go-between, the emissary, was lost to the wild throngings of civilization, poisoned, stolen, hit by a car, left somewhere in a culvert. . . .

Sobbing, Martin turned his face to his pillow. The world was a picture under glass, untouchable. The world was dead.

▶ In what sense was Martin's world dead?
▶ Are there any clues to Dog's change of behaviour?
▶ How is the tone of the story changing?

Martin twisted in bed and in three days the last Hallowe'en pumpkins were rotting in trash cans, papier-mâché skulls and witches were burnt on bonfires, and ghosts were stacked on shelves with other linens until next year.

To Martin, Hallowe'en had been nothing more than one evening when tin horns cried off in the cold autumn stars, children blew like goblin leaves along the flinty walks, flinging their heads, or cabbages, at porches, soap-writing names or similar magic symbols on icy windows. All of it as distant, unfathomable, and nightmarish as a puppet show seen from so many miles away that there is no sound or meaning.

For three days in November, Martin watched alternate light and shadow sift across his ceiling. The fire-pageant was over forever; autumn lay in cold ashes. Martin sank deeper, yet deeper in white marble layers of bed, motionless, listening always listening. . . .

Friday evening, his parents kissed him good-night and walked out of the house into the hushed cathedral weather toward a motion-picture show. Miss Tarkin from next door stayed on in the parlour below until Martin called down he was sleepy, then took her knitting off home.

In silence, Martin lay following the great move of stars down a clear and moonlit sky, remembering nights such as this when he'd spanned the town with Dog ahead, behind, around about, tracking the green-plush ravine, lapping slumbrous streams gone milky with the fullness of the moon, leaping cemetery tombstones while whispering the marble names; on, quickly on, through shaved meadows where the only motion was the off-on quivering of stars, to streets where shadows would not stand aside for you but crowded all the sidewalks for mile on mile. Run now run! chasing, being chased by bitter smoke, fog, mist, wind, ghost of mind, fright of memory; home, safe, sound, snug-warm, asleep. . . .

Nine o'clock.

Chime. The drowsy clock in the deep stairwell below. Chime.

Dog, come home, and run the world with you. Dog, bring a thistle with frost on it, or bring nothing else but the wind. Dog, where *are* you? Oh, listen, now, I'll call.

Martin held his breath.

Way off somewhere — a sound.

Martin rose up, trembling.

There, again — the sound.

So small a sound, like a sharp needle-point brushing the sky long miles and many miles away.

The dreamy echo of a dog — barking.

The sound of a dog crossing fields and farms, dirt roads and rabbit paths, running, running, letting out great barks of steam, cracking the night. The sound of a circling dog which came and went, lifted and faded, opened up, shut in, moved forward, went back, as if the animal were kept by someone on a fantastically long chain. As if the dog were running and someone whistled under the chestnut trees, in mould-shadow, tar-shadow, moon-shadow, walking, and the dog circled back and sprang out again towards home.

Dog! Martin thought, oh Dog, come home, boy! Listen, oh, listen, where you *been*? Come on, boy, make tracks!

Five, ten, fifteen minutes; near, very near, the bark, the sound. Martin cried out, thrust his feet from the bed, leaned to the window. Dog! Listen, boy! Dog! Dog! He said it over and over. Dog! Dog! Wicked Dog, run off and gone all these days! Bad Dog, good Dog, home, boy, hurry, and bring what you can!

Near now, near, up the street, barking, to knock clapboard housefronts with sound, whirl iron cocks on rooftops in the moon, firing off volleys — Dog! now at the door below. . . .

Martin shivered.

Should he run — let Dog in, or wait for Mom and Dad? Wait? Oh, God, wait? But what if Dog ran off again? No, he'd go down, snatch the door wide, yell, grab Dog in, and run upstairs so fast, laughing, crying, holding tight, that . . .

Dog stopped barking.

Hey! Martin almost broke the window, jerking to it.

Silence. As if someone had told Dog to hush now, hush, hush.

A full minute passed. Martin clenched his fists.

Below, a faint whimpering.

Then, slowly, the downstairs front door opened. Someone was kind enough to have opened the door for Dog. Of course! Dog had brought Mr Jacobs or Mr Gillespie or Miss Tarkins, or . . .

The downstairs door shut.

Dog raced upstairs, whining, flung himself on the bed.

'Dog, Dog, where've you *been*, what've you *done*! Dog, Dog!'

And he crushed Dog hard and long to himself, weeping. Dog, Dog. He laughed and shouted. Dog! But after a moment he stopped laughing and crying, suddenly.

He pulled away. He held the animal and looked at him, eyes widening.

The odour coming from Dog was different.

It was a smell of strange earth. It was a smell of night within night, the smell of digging down deep in shadow through earth that had lain cheek by jowl with things that were long hidden and decayed. A stinking and rancid soil fell away in clods of dissolution from Dog's muzzle and paws. He had dug deep. He had dug very deep indeed. That *was* it, wasn't it? wasn't it? *wasn't* it!

What kind of message was this from Dog? What could such a message mean? The stench — the ripe and awful cemetery earth.

Dog was a bad dog, digging where he shouldn't. Dog was a good dog, always making friends. Dog loved people. Dog brought them home.

And now, moving up the dark hall stairs, at intervals, came the sound of feet, one foot dragged after the other, painfully, slowly, slowly, slowly.

Dog shivered. A rain of strange night earth fell seething on the bed.

Dog turned.

The bedroom door whispered in.

Martin had company.

Ray Bradbury

Looking back

▶ What techniques and language did the writer use to create the tension for the climax of this story. For example: Hallowe'en, Martin alone in the house, echoes of a dog barking, the chime of a clock.

▶ At what moment were you finally convinced that the story had developed into a ghost, or supernatural story? What made you realize the story had changed?

Extra ideas

Some newspapers report at length on personal dramas such as this. Imagine you are an investigative journalist working for such a paper. Write a sensational account of the events in this story.

You can imagine this story being turned into a successful film. Imagine you wanted to persuade a film company to give you the money to make the film. Write a statement that has:
▶ a brief outline of the story
▶ reference to scenes you would expand, reduce, create or leave out
▶ special effects needed
▶ preferred actors and actresses for the parts
▶ your intended audience.

Three very short stories

Here are three very short stories. There are differences and similarities between them, so you will find suggestions for talking and writing about each one individually and about all of them, as a whole.

Looking ahead

Before reading the story, make a list of all the occasions when you might give or send someone flowers. Are they happy or sad occasions?

The story has nine paragraphs. Although numbers one and nine are in the right place, the others have been mixed up. Reconstruct the story in an order which produces a satisfying narrative for you.

You should find the early paragraphs convey a relaxed, happy atmosphere and the tone begins to change with the one starting 'By twelve o'clock'.

Compare your sequence with that of another pair or group.

The Flowers

1

It seemed to Myop as she skipped lightly from hen house to pigpen to smokehouse that the days had never been as beautiful as these. The air held a keenness that made her nose twitch. The harvesting of the corn and cotton, peanuts and squash, made each day a golden surprise that caused excited little tremors to run up her jaws.

Myop carried a short, knobby stick. She struck out at random at chickens she liked, and worked out the beat of a song on the fence around the pigpen. She felt light and good in the warm sun. She was ten, and nothing existed for her but her song, the stick clutched in her dark brown hand, and the tat-de-ta-ta-ta of accompaniment.

She had explored the woods behind the house many times. Often, in late autumn, her mother took her to gather nuts among the fallen leaves. Today she made her own path, bouncing this way and that way, vaguely keeping an eye out for snakes. She found, in addition to various common but pretty ferns and leaves, an armful of strange blue flowers with velvety ridges and a sweetsuds bush full of the brown, fragrant buds.

Myop gazed around the spot with interest. Very near where she'd stepped into the head was a wild pink rose. As she picked it to add to her bundle she noticed a raised mound, a ring, around the rose's root. It was the rotted remains of a noose, a bit of shredding ploughline, now blending benignly into the soil. Around an overhanging limb of a great spreading oak clung another piece. Frayed, rotted, bleached, and frazzled — barely there — but spinning restlessly in the breeze. Myop laid down her flowers.

Turning her back on the rusty boards of her family's sharecropper cabin, Myop walked along the fence till it ran into the stream made by the spring. Around the spring, where the family got drinking water, silver ferns and wildflowers grew. Along the shallow banks pigs rooted. Myop watched the tiny white bubbles disrupt the thin black scale of soil and the water that silently rose and slid away down the stream.

Myop began to circle back to the house, back to the peacefulness of the morning. It was then she stepped smack into his eyes. Her heel became lodged in the broken ridge between brow and nose, and she reached down quickly, unafraid, to free herself. It was only when she saw his naked grin that she gave a little yelp of surprise.

By twelve o'clock, her arms laden with sprigs of her findings, she was a mile or more from home. She had often been as far before, but the strangeness of the land made it not as pleasant as her usual haunts. It seemed gloomy in the little cove in which she found herself. The air was damp, the silence close and deep.

9

And the summer was over.

He had been a tall man. From feet to neck covered a long space. His head lay beside him. When she pushed back the leaves and layers of earth and debris Myop saw that he'd had large white teeth, all of them cracked or broken, long fingers, and very big bones. All his clothes had rotted away except some threads of blue denim from his overalls. The buckles of the overalls had turned green.

The writer's version of the story is on page 77.

Looking back

When you have reconstructed the story and reread it, decide which of the following statements you agree with and why. You will need to discuss them in groups.

▶ Myop wanted to explore the woods for herself that day.
▶ Myop was short-sighted, as her name suggests.
▶ Myop was frightened when she saw the skull.
▶ Myop understood the significance of the rope.
▶ Myop laid down her flowers as a mark of respect.
▶ The last line refers to a change in the weather.

Myop seems to have an awareness of what the rope signified. Are there other dangers in the wood that she should have been aware of? What do you think is the theme of this story?

Extra ideas

▶ Imagine Myop keeps a diary. She has room for 100 words. What would she write in her diary for that day?
▶ Write your own story in which a walk in the country or in the city leads to an important discovery.
▶ Write from your own personal experience of an event that helped or forced you to grow up.

Looking ahead

People make telephone calls for many reasons. Does the first sentence of the next story suggest a reason for the call?

Telephone Call

The door opened for a moment and some of Mrs Prince's grief escaped, bolting with the tomcat into the backyard. Then Fanny came out, closed the door, and walked slowly down the steps. Mrs Jacobs, scrubbing clothes on the other porch, looked at her. The crazy boy's mother, Mrs Savini looked at her. Even old Mrs Jackson, the deaf *schwartzer*, heard something and looked up.

'Is mama sick?' Mrs Jacobs asked.

'No,' Fanny said, 'Mrs Jacobs,' she wet her lips, 'mama says kin she please borrow a nickel till Saturday?'

Mrs Jacobs was immediately and intensely embarrassed. 'I ain't got not a penny in the house,' she wailed. 'May I die if I got one penny even.'

Men from the fire-station had water-hoses trained on Ethel and Sarah and the other children. 'Come on, Fanny! Come on!' they shouted as she passed. It was a very hot day and on such days there was no greater fun than 'swimming in air through water,' as this game was called. It was better even than ice cream or all-day suckers. 'I can't,' Fanny said, 'I got to call on the telephone.' She dodged but got a little bit wet.

Mr Smolefsky's face was pitted like a bad apple. His daughter sang love songs at the school affairs, and she was also in the store.

'A nickel, huh!' Mr Smolefsky said. 'Why not a dollar or ten dollars? You people sure got your nerve.'

'We ain't runnin' no grocery business for charity,' his daughter shrilled. 'Tell your ma she should settle what she owes first.'

The drug store boss was in the back, joking with someone. The clerk was waiting on trade.

'What is it, little girl?' he asked at last.

'My mama says kin you please lend us a nickel for the telephone. My mama wants to call up my daddy. He stays at the City Relief Farm. My daddy's name is Mr Prince.'

The clerk frowned.

'All right,' he said.

Fanny watched him dial the number.

'Hello. City Farm? Let me talk to Mr Prince. P-r-i-n-c-e. Prince. . . . What's his first name, little girl? . . . Abe. A-b-e. He's one of the workers, I guess. Yeah, she says it's important. . . . Hello, Abe? Just a minute. . . .'

Fanny craned her neck. 'Hello, daddy dear. This is Fanny talking. Mama says come home right away. The baby won't wake up. . . . Can you hear me, daddy? . . . The baby —'

She burst into tears and the clerk had to finish the conversation for her.

J. S. Balch

 ▶ Some adults would say that this story is not suitable for young people. What thoughts or emotions did it generate for you? Write an opinion in response to an adult who says, 'It's too old for you to read.'

Looking back

When you have read the story once, reread it and note down the characters whom Fanny meets. Beside each name record (a) what evidence there was that all was not well with Fanny and (b) what each might have done to help.

NAME	EVIDENCE OF FANNY'S DISTRESS	HELP THAT COULD HAVE BEEN GIVEN

Extra ideas

What can the Prince family do? Write a short play which might cover the arrival home of Abe Prince and some of the following suggestions:
▶ the talk with his wife and Fanny
▶ the confronting of Mr Smolefsky
▶ a decision as to what to do for the future.
(You could write this as a group)

Compare and contrast this story with 'The Flowers', or 'I Used to Live Here Once'. Use the subheadings under 'Writing a review' on page 76 to help you and say which story you preferred.

This next story is set in Dominica, in the Caribbean.

I Used to Live Here Once

She was standing by the river looking at the stepping stones and remembering each one. There was the round unsteady stone, the pointed one, the flat one in the middle — the safe stone where you could stand and look around. The next wasn't so safe for when the river was full the water flowed over it and even when it showed dry it was slippery. But after that it was easy and soon she was standing on the other side.

The road was much wider than it used to be but the work had been done carelessly. The felled trees had not been cleared away and the bushes looked trampled. Yet it was the same road and she walked along feeling extraordinarily happy.

It was a fine day, a blue day. The only thing was that the sky had a glassy look that she didn't remember. That was the only word she could think of. Glassy. She turned the corner, saw that what had been the old pavé had been taken up, and there too the road was much wider, but it had the same unfinished look.

She came to the worn stone steps that led up to the house and her heart began to beat. The screw pine was gone, so was the mock summer house called the ajoupa, but the clove tree was still there and at the top of the steps the rough lawn stretched away, just as she remembered it. She stopped and looked towards the house that had been added to and painted white. It was strange to see a car standing in front of it.

There were two children under the big mango tree, a boy and a little girl, and she waved to them and called 'Hello' but they didn't answer her or turn their heads. Very fair children, as Europeans born in the West Indies so often are: as if the white blood is asserting itself against all odds.

The grass was yellow in the hot sunlight as she walked towards them. When she was quite close she called again, shyly: 'Hello'. Then, 'I used to live here once,' she said.

Still they didn't answer. When she said for the third time 'Hello' she was quite near them. Her arms went out instinctively with the longing to touch them.

It was the boy who turned. His grey eyes looked straight into hers. His expression didn't change. He said 'Hasn't it gone cold all of a sudden. D'you notice? Let's go in.' 'Yes let's' said the girl.

Her arms fell to her sides as she watched them running across the grass to the house. That was the first time she knew.

Jean Rhys

Looking back

 When you have read the story, discuss the following questions:

▶ 'That was the first time she knew'. What did she now know?
▶ What possible reasons could there be to explain the behaviour of the fair children?
▶ Could the story be set in any country?
▶ What hopes would you have if you went back to visit a place you had previously lived in?
▶ Make a chart with two columns and list all the similarities and differences the girl mentions as she describes the place she has come back to visit.

Extra ideas

Write your own story about returning to a place you once knew well. Describe your expectations before arriving, your feelings on discovering the familiar and the unfamiliar, your thoughts on leaving again. You could use the title: 'I Used to Live Here Once'.

The story is written in the third person. Imagine an ex-pupil returns to your school. Describe his or her observations of your school as it is now and as it used to be.

Writing a review

You might want to write a review of one of the stories you have read in this unit, or another story that you have read. These are some of the aspects of a short story that you should consider:

The title and the author.
▶ Do you know when the story was written and is this relevant to understanding the story?

Where and when the story is set.

A brief summary of the plot.
▶ What happens in the story and who or what is involved?
▶ What is the main character like?

The style and structure of the story.
▶ Who tells the story? Is it first or third-person narrative?
▶ What is the language like? Is there dialogue?
▶ What is the atmosphere of the story and does it change?
▶ Is there tension, or a climax?
▶ Is there an unexpected ending?

The type of story, or genre.
▶ What features does the story have to suit the genre?

The theme of the story.
▶ What is the main theme of the story? Does the story carry a message?

Your opinion.

▶ Did you like the story?

▶ Were you moved, affected, stimulated by it?

▶ What did you think about after reading it?

▶ Would you recommend it, and if so, to whom?

The Flowers

It seemed to Myop as she skipped lightly from hen house to pigpen to smokehouse that the days had never been as beautiful as these. The air held a keenness that made her nose twitch. The harvesting of the corn and cotton, peanuts and squash, made each day a golden surprise that caused excited little tremors to run up her jaws.

Myop carried a short, knobby stick. She struck out at random at chickens she liked, and worked out the beat of a song on the fence around the pigpen. She felt light and good in the warm sun. She was ten, and nothing existed for her but her song, the stick clutched in her dark brown hand, and the tat-de-ta-ta-ta of accompaniment.

Turning her back on the rusty boards of her family's sharecropper cabin, Myop walked along the fence till it ran into the stream made by the spring. Around the spring, where the family got drinking water, silver ferns and wild-flowers grew. Along the shallow banks pigs rooted. Myop watched the tiny white bubbles disrupt the thin black scale of soil and the water that silently rose and slid away down the stream.

She had explored the woods behind the house many times. Often, in late autumn, her mother took her to gather nuts among the fallen leaves. Today she made her own path, bouncing this way and that way, vaguely keeping an eye out for snakes. She found, in addition to various common but pretty ferns and leaves, an armful of strange blue flowers with velvety ridges and a sweetsuds bush full of the brown, fragrant buds.

By twelve o'clock, her arms laden with sprigs of her findings, she was a mile or more from home. She had often been as far before, but the strangeness of the land made it not as pleasant as her usual haunts. It seemed gloomy in the little cove in which she found herself. The air was damp, the silence close and deep.

Myop began to circle back to the house, back to the peacefulness of the morning. It was then she stepped smack into his eyes. Her heel became lodged in the broken ridge between brow and nose, and she reached down quickly, unafraid, to free herself. It was only when she saw his naked grin that she gave a little yelp of surprise.

He had been a tall man. From feet to neck covered a long space. His head lay beside him. When she pushed back the leaves and layers of earth and debris Myop saw that he'd had large white teeth, all of them cracked or broken, long fingers, and very big bones. All his clothes had rotted away except some threads of blue denim from his overalls. The buckles of the overalls had turned green.

Myop gazed around the spot with interest. Very near where she'd stepped into the head was a wild pink rose. As she picked it to add to her bundle she noticed a raised mound, a ring, around the rose's root. It was the rotted remains of a noose, a bit of shredding ploughline, now blending benignly into the soil. Around an overhanging limb of a great spreading oak clung another piece. Frayed, rotted, bleached, and frazzled — barely there — but spinning restlessly in the breeze. Myop laid down her flowers.

And the summer was over.

Alice Walker

6

WRITING FOR YOUR RIGHTS

IN THIS UNIT YOU WILL WORK OUT HOW TO ORGANISE A CAMPAIGN IN YOUR LOCAL AREA BY COLLECTING INFORMATION, DISCUSSING THE ISSUES, WRITING LETTERS, AND MAKING POSTERS AND LEAFLETS.

Safety campaign

Narrow Escape for Schoolboy

A minicab driver appeared at Shawcross Magistrates' Court on Friday charged with dangerous driving. John Wilson (36) of Sherbourne Avenue, Morton, knocked down thirteen-year-old Peter Thomas as he was returning home from school at 4.30 on Thursday 21 March. Wilson, an experienced driver, stated that visibility was poor and the boy rushed across the road in front of him. 'I didn't have a chance,' he said. From his hospital bed, Peter Thomas, who sustained a broken leg, said, 'That's always been a dangerous place. There have been loads of accidents when kids are rushing to catch the train.'

Wilson was fined £100, and ordered to pay £75 damages. His licence was endorsed for one year.

At registration time on Monday 25 March, Peter Thomas's form talk about the accident with their teacher. Here is a transcript of their discussion.

JEAN: How long's he going to be in then?

HASSAD: Er, about two weeks at least. His Mum said it's a bad break so he'll have to have it in plaster for at least a month.

CHARLIE: That means we've had it for the game against Paisley.

JEAN: You boys. You're all the same. All you think of is football. What about Peter? He's going to be stuck in plaster for ages. And what about the other kids that have been hurt there. Yeah my cousin nearly got knocked over last week and she wasn't even running.

HASSAD: It's when the cars come round that corner.

TEACHER: Well you've been told time and again that you should cross at the traffic lights.

CHARLIE: But if you cut across the Green that saves you going right back to the main road.

TEACHER: That is not the point when lives are at stake.

JEAN: Well I think they should put a zebra crossing there. Why should we have to walk all the way round in the rain. . . .

It wasn't long before the class had decided to organise their own 'Zebra-Crossing' campaign in an effort to prove to the local council that a crossing was needed. First they drew a plan of the area round the school and marked on it the different routes taken by the pupils going to and from school.

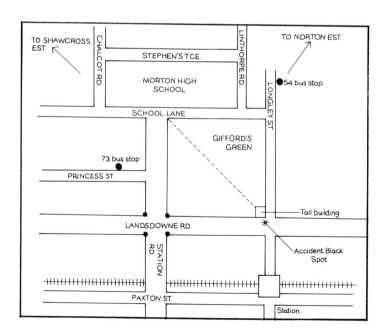

The next stage was to gather information about the number of pupils who used the routes. They made up a simple questionnaire for this.

Name: _____

Form: _____

Age: _____

Do you go to school by: Train   ☐

                         Bus   ☐

                     73 Bus   ☐

                     54 Bus   ☐

                     Walk   ☐

If you walk do you come from: Shawcross Est ☐

                                 Morton ☐

                         South of the railway. ☐

The questionnaire revealed the following facts: out of 800 pupils
▶ 200 travel to school by train
▶ 100 use 73 bus
▶ 50 use 54 bus
▶ 450 walk to school.

Of those who walk
▶ 100 come from Shawcross
▶ 150 come from South of the railway
▶ 200 come from Morton.
(All of these figures have been rounded up or down to the nearest fifty.)

Finally they sent this letter to the local paper.

Class 4B,
Morton High School,
Stephen's Terrace,
Shawcross,
6JR 2NB.
27/3/89

The Editor,
Shawcross Gazette,
106, High St.,
Manchester 8.

Dear Editor,
        On 21 March Peter Thomas, a second-year pupil at Morton High, was knocked down and seriously injured as he crossed Landsdowne Road on his way home from school. This is not the first accident of its kind and we are convinced it will not be the last unless a zebra crossing is installed.
        Up to 350 pupils cross Landsdowne Road twice daily going to and from the station and school. They nearly always take the short cut across Gifford's Green and you can't stop them doing this.
        We are certain that parents and other members of the public must be as concerned as we are about this accident black-spot and we appeal to all your readers to support our zebra campaign by writing to local councillors asking for urgent action to be taken.
        Yours sincerely

        Class 4B, Morton High School

Building your own campaign

You now have the facts. In groups or in pairs you are going to continue 4B's campaign. You will need to carry out the following tasks:
► Decide on a slogan for the campaign.
► Design a logo — a small drawing that will appear on all publicity and should become instantly recognisable as the campaign symbol.
► Write a letter to the local primary school asking for support for the campaign. The letter will have the same information and layout as

the letter to the paper but you will have to change the language to suit young children. You will be trying to persuade the children to join your campaign.

▶ Design a poster or a leaflet for your campaign:

   (i) Poster: this should be designed for the wall so the information must be clear and easily understood. Most of it will be visual but words will be important as well.

   (ii) Leaflet: this will probably be folded A4 paper with an eye-catching front page but with plenty of informative writing, bar-charts and maps inside.

 ▶ Prepare a two-to-five-minute presentation for the school assembly about the campaign.

Now you have prepared an imaginary campaign, see if there is a real issue in your school or local area that your group or class would like to take on. Local issues tend to be things like this:

▶ school rules or facilities

▶ adventure playground threatened

▶ more play-space needed for young children

▶ swimming pool needed

- ▶ bike sheds in school
- ▶ anti-litter and graffiti campaign in school
- ▶ pollution of local river
- ▶ post office/library closure
- ▶ racial harassment on local estate.

To find out what people in your area are concerned about:
1. Read two or three issues of the local paper, particularly the letters page.
2. Visit the local Citizens Advice Bureau or Community Centre.
3. Go to the public library and read the notice board giving details of public meetings.
4. Ask the people you know — friends, relations, and neighbours — what concerns them about living in the area. Try to include an elderly person, a parent of young children, an unemployed person, a teenager, and so on.

To find out what the issues are in school, you will have to carry out a survey amongst older or younger pupils as well as your own age group.

When you have decided what your campaign is to be about, plan your action to include the following tasks.
- ▶ a slogan
- ▶ a logo
- ▶ letters to newspapers, local councillors, primary schools, youth clubs, churches and other community groups
- ▶ surveys
- ▶ posters and publicity leaflets.

At some stage try to present your campaign to a wider audience, e.g. another class, a primary school, a school assembly, or a parents' meeting.

7

THE PROFESSIONALS

STUDYING AN AUTHOR

At some time in your course you will probably have to choose a literature topic to study on your own. It could be:
▶ a study of a writer
▶ a study of a theme such as 'Children in Books'
▶ a study of a genre such as Science Fiction
▶ a study of the literature of a particular period such as 'Poetry of the First World War'.

In this unit you will see how to go about preparing a study on Robert Leeson, a professional writer of books for children. There will be a number of tasks that will result in a written 'author' study. You may want to write about Robert Leeson, or to work on a writer of your own choice following the method used here.

Robert Leeson: in his own words

▶ Starting out

I was brought up in a village in Cheshire overlooking a valley where there was a huge chemical factory employing 20,000 people. Everybody else worked on the surrounding farms. It was that borderland between town and country that has produced many writers. Our parents were fanatical about education and were absolutely determined that their four children should get the education they had been denied. The four of us passed the scholarship to go to the local Grammar school which was remarkable when you think that only one in thirty kids managed it. There they made tremendous efforts to rid us of our local dialect, to stop us talking as our parents did. So, like most kids we learned two or three ways of talking. That was the bad side. The good thing was that I had an English teacher who encouraged me to write. He never rejected the stories I wrote when I had been given an essay to do and he sometimes let me read them out to the class. The result was that by the time I was fourteen I had written two novels and by the time I left school at sixteen I was determined to be a writer.

Because of the war there were vacancies on the local paper so I started off as a junior reporter but after eighteen months I had to join the army myself. When I returned to civilian life there was no place for me on the paper so I worked for a time on the canals and for the Co-Op. Then I was offered a job working for an international youth magazine in Belgrade and I've earned my living as a writer ever since. I went freelance in 1969.

Over the past thirteen years I have written 27 novels and 24 have been published or are about to be. I think the process of writing is like dreaming. What happens when you dream is that the raw material which has entered the mind at different times — maybe ten minutes ago or ten years ago — is absorbed into the subconscious and is restructured. In dreams you get familiar figures portrayed naturally or in a fantastic way and what appear to be strangers are in fact inventions of the mind based upon the people you have met but have forgotten. Writing is a bit like that. Ideas appear from nowhere but they must be reprocessed and it can take a long time. I was writing for thirty years before I got any fiction published. The idea for *The Third Class Genie*, the idea of someone invisible in a tin, first came to me when I was about ten and had heard a radio serial based upon *The Invisible Man* by H. G. Wells. But I did not do anything with it because the idea was just a reflection of something I'd been listening to. It remained in my head for over thirty years when I had another impulse in which I remembered a film I saw when I was a kid called Alfie's Button about somebody who'd got a button that was part of Aladdin's lamp. Now put the two together and that is what I call an idea: a magic working genie inside a beercan.

▶ *How I write*

What I do first of all when I have an idea is wait. Then I assist the waiting by using a notebook which I carry around with me all the time and in which I simply note ideas. I don't sit writing down what the people next to me on the bus or train are saying and I certainly do not lurk around schools eavesdropping on teachers and kids. What goes into my notebook is what comes out of my head reprocessed; not what people put there. Once the idea has been accepted the whole process will last about nine months or a year. For the first six months I work on notes testing out the story and the plot. If it seems there are major problems I may abandon the idea. When I decide it is time for me to plan the plot in detail then I am totally committed to the book and for about two months I plan the book in minute detail on large sheets of paper. This is a necessary process which is especially important for aspiring writers. If it is ignored it will result in a lot of frustration or even failure. A story can be made to work by planning. Lack of planning, simply forging ahead, may lead to the writer running out of puff. There is an important difference between readers and writers. For the reader it's like opening the book and following a path that has been prepared by the writer. You don't question how the path came to be there — you just walk on. The process of writing, however, is like creating a map or a landscape, setting the path for the reader to follow through the landscape. The reader is only aware of the path but the writer must know every detail of the landscape even though it may not be visible to the reader at the time.

When the planning period is over I move to the final stage. I write very

swiftly now. For example I wrote *Silver's Revenge* in eight days, that is I physically wrote 54,000 words in that time. My ideal situation is to work as swiftly as possible with very few changes or corrections when I feel I have the whole story in my head and am telling it to an unseen audience. Very often what I do in the final stage is to write the first few chapters in longhand and I may in fact write the first page several times discarding and changing. But once I am confident that the story is coming out right I get on to the typewriter and very often it is that typescript that goes to the publisher almost without correction.

I am always writing. I try to work regular hours from 9.0 to about 4.30 with a break in the middle. When I finish a book I need a bit of a rest. It's quite wearing and often I lose a bit of weight. So I take a break for a month or two, when I will visit schools and give talks about writing. And while this is going on the first stages of other books will be in preparation.

I am often told by editors that I have made peculiar spelling errors but I'm not conscious of them. I think my spelling is almost immaculate. In *The Third Class Genie* I wrote 'camel' every time I meant to write 'canal', I don't know if you'd call that a mistake. I also consistently write 'their' when I mean to write 'there' but it's purely carelessness. I think children are picked up in school for spelling mistakes when they know perfectly well how to spell. A perfectly intelligent kid makes some stupid spelling mistake over and over again and a great big fuss is made of it. I can go over a typescript three or four times and each time I find mistakes.

▶ *My audience*

From the very first book I have become much more conscious of the audience and the need to see writing as a dialogue between the writer and the reader. There are certain things you want to say and when you're writing for younger children, certain things you may not be able to say. I have become more and more aware of the role of the audience, the importance of the audience and the rights of the reader. The beauty of being a writer of literature for children is that you have an audience of eight- to eighteen-year-olds. There is a tremendous development of understanding in those years. On the one hand small children who are only just becoming independent readers and on the other people who have boy and girl friends, driving licences and the vote. There is room here for a tremendous range of ideas and thoughts and word-pictures. But whatever age they are they want to hear what you say clearly and truthfully. You've got to treat the person you're writing for with the respect of believing that they know what you're talking about. In other words you don't talk down to somebody just because they're younger. At the same time you have to accept that there are certain things you can talk about which may be outside their experience. So you are constantly having to readjust the notion of how the audience is listening — accepting, absorbing or agreeing with what you want to say.

Strictly speaking I don't really care what the critics say about my writing but if the kids don't want to read my books then I must seriously ask what I'm in the business for. I am happy for my books to be judged by the class-reader test, that is, the teachers like to teach them and the kids like to read them.

How an author works

One of Robert Leeson's many popular books is *Grange Hill Rules O.K.* Here we give the first page as it appeared in print together with the manuscript that Robert Leeson wrote. We also include some of the notes he made for the first chapter and some character notes.

A story can be made to work by planning. Lack of planning, simply forging ahead, may lead to a writer running out of puff.

For about two months I plan the book in minute detail on large sheets of paper.

Tucker	Benny	Doyle	Justin
Keep out of trouble	Newspaper round	Planning Doyle's	Father wants
Building Site	Dad still ill.	destruction	him in grammar-
Silence compo	In with Tucker on	- Plan A.	Mother not -
Seized by Doyle	Building Site.	Suggesting idea	her job in question?
Building Site 2.	In with Tucker	of semolina to	He not certain
In danger of exp.	on wheelchair	Trisha	what he wants
Nicking wheelchair	episode.		but doesn't
Rescuing Cathy	Wants to buy	Getting Tucker by	want to be
Adventure with	Christmas present.	Staffroom.	disturbed.
wheelchair		Putting up Robbo's	Research on
& Justin		Dad on Parent	project
[Trouble with Justin]		ticket	Old lady with
Helping Benny		Alder kids sorted	wheelchair
on Newspapers.		out!	Official
		Ten shopping	recounts - dull
		days to Xmas	as ditch water.
			He now spends
		Gets publicity	time in her
		for Trishe's	house.
		semolina.	Late home etc.
			Father getting
			annoyed.
			He finds
			wheelchair
			removed —
			Shed etc.
			Chases them —
			fight etc
			The wheelchair
			race.

I may in fact write the first page
several times, discarding and changing.

0700 hours on a cold December
morning 20 schooling days to
Xmas and the Magnificent 7
of Grange Hill County were still
wrapped up in their blanket rolls.

No! One was awake. Little
Benny Green had his clothes on
and was sneaking down stairs
Mum left for work 20 mins ago.
Dad had been up half the
night with his head but now
he's asleep.

Benny had discussed a way of
earning some much needed pocket
money. But just for the moment
he was keeping it to himself
As he reached the new road he passed
a parked car. He took no notice of
the man at the wheel but the
driver took note of him.
B. Green was being watched but
d no it.

0800 hours. Penny Lewis chewed toast
and marmalade as she went over
her notes for the 2nd year assembley
that day. The School Council had

decided on a long charity Sponsored walk – in competition with B. School. Penny wondered for the 10th time what the 2nd year would say when she put the idea to them. Peter Jenkins would object. If there was one thing he hated more than walking it was organised walking.

Tricia Yates would object as well. Because just lately everything Penny said or did seemed to get right up Tricia's nose. Penny shrugged and stuffed her note into her bag. 20 mins later she was in the car passing through the shopping centre on the way to school. Suddenly her mother braked & swung the car to the kerb.

"Look there's that sweet little Justin Bennett – lets give him a lift."

The finished product

Chapter 1

0700 hours on a cold December morning and the Magnificent Seven of Grange Hill were still wrapped in their blanket rolls.

No! One was awake. Little Benny Green had his clothes on and was creeping downstairs. Mum left for work twenty minutes ago. Dad had been up half the night with his back, but now was asleep at last. Benny had found a way of earning some much needed pocket money. But he was keeping it to himself for the moment.

As he reached the main road, heading for the shops, he passed a parked car. The man at the wheel took careful note of him as he went by.

0800 hours. Penny Templeton Lewis chewed toast and marmalade as she went over her notes for the Year Assembly that morning. The School Council had decided on a big charity sponsored walk — in competition with Brookdale School. For the tenth time, Penny wondered what they'd all say when she put the idea to them. Peter Jenkins would object — naturally. If there was one thing he hated more than walking, it was organized walking. Trisha Yates would object, too. Just lately everything Penny said or did seemed to get right up Trisha's nose. Penny shrugged and stuffed her notes into her bag.

Twenty minutes later, she was in the car, passing through the shopping centre on the way to school. Suddenly her mother braked and swung the car to the kerb.

'Look, there's that sweet little Justin Bennett. Let's give him a lift.'

Your author study

1. Part of your writing should include some information about the author you are studying. In the case of Robert Leeson the information came from an interview with the writer but, more often than not, you will have to do some library-based research. You will have to consult magazine articles, newspaper cuttings, and reference books which give biographies of writers. There may be videos that are helpful.

When you are deciding which author to study always bear in mind the availability of books and other library resources. When you have made your notes it will help to focus on what to include in the final written work by actually giving a talk to your group or, if that is not possible, imagine you are the presenter of a book programme for eleven- to fourteen-year-olds. One of your programmes will include a five-minute spot on Robert Leeson, introducing the writer and his books to the teenage audience. Use the information in this section to prepare the start of the programme. You could begin with a quotation such as:

'I am happy for my books to be judged by the class-reader test, that is the teachers like to teach them and the kids like to read them.' This is the down-to-earth approach that has made Bob Leeson so popular with his readers . . .

2. You have found out some background information about your author. Now you have to study the books themselves.

Readers often take book covers and publishers' 'blurbs' for granted but intense thought and care go into the packaging of a book. The illustration has to summarise the book visually just as the 'blurb' makes a summary in words. It can be a useful introduction to a writer to study the book covers and see how the publisher has projected the author's work.

Here are two book covers and the 'blurbs' that appear on the back of each book.

Patty Bergen is a young Jewish girl in Jacksonville, Arkansas, in the early 1940s. Treated harshly by her father, and shown little affection by her mother, Patty finds most comfort in the warm kindness of the family's black servant, Ruth. When a German prisoner-of-war, Anton Reiker, escapes from a local camp, Patty forges an extraordinary friendship across racial and patriotic divides. In a situation fraught with danger, only Ruth is to be trusted with Patty's secret.

This moving and compassionate story of the Second World War in America's Deep South is full of action and interest. It is concerned with prejudice and bigotry, on the one side, against sympathy and human understanding, on the other. In Anton's words, 'I believe that love is better than hate'.

A new supermarket which has replaced an old-fashioned grocer's is plagued by mysterious happenings—who does the voice over the tannoy belong to?

Plates fly across the room and are smashed in a large family home—what is going on?

A girl with none of her twin sister's talent for singing and dancing suddenly gains it—but where from?

A boy ridicules a classmate's talk of magic, yet has a shocking experience himself . . .

In these scary stories Lance Salway writes about ordinary girls and boys—and the *extra*ordinary things that can happen to them when the 'ghosties and ghoulies' take over. The most innocent situations become sinister, the most normal turn nasty. Fortunately there's comedy too: some of the ghosts have a sense of humour!

As a preliminary exercise make a list of the books starting with the one you would like to read most, *based on the evidence of the covers*. Work your way down the list to the one you would least like to read. After discussing your preferences with other people write down your reasons for putting the books in that order.

At this stage, before you have actually read any books, you may be able to find out more about individual titles by talking to people who have read them.

3. Your final writing could be done on your own or in a group. Besides putting your work in your personal folder, you may like to enlarge your audience by making a wall display or preparing a folder for the library.

4. Now you must select some titles to read. Be realistic with regard to the time you have and the length of the books. Remember you cannot always rely on libraries to provide popular books without a two- to three-week wait.

The following list of popular children's writers might be useful:

Joan Aiken	Julius Lester
Bernard Ashley	Joan Lingard
Nina Bawden	Jan Mark
Judy Blume	Terry Nation
Betsy Byars	Jan Needle
Susan Cooper	Katherine Paterson
Roald Dahl	Jill Paton-Walsh
Marjorie Darke	Philippa Pearce
Anita Desai	David Rees
Farrukh Dhondy	Ian Serraillier
Peter Dickinson	Rosemary Sutcliff
Buchi Emecheta	Robert Swindells
Nicholas Fisk	John Rowe Townsend
Alan Garner	Sue Townsend
Rosa Guy	Jean Ure
Gene Kemp	Robert Westall
Tim Kennemore	Paul Zindel
Robert Leeson	

(You may want to choose an author of your own who is not on this list.)

Preparation

▶ Make a list of all the titles by the writer you have chosen. Photo-copy covers if possible.

▶ Make notes on any of your writer's books that you have already read.

▶ Read at least two of the books. If you are working in a group share out the titles.

▶ Find out if it is possible to contact your writer. This is usually done through the publishers.

▶ Prepare a list of questions to be included in a letter to your writer.

▶ Research information for a biography. Consult your librarian for magazine articles.

The final folder

This should include some of the following items:

▶ An attractive layout of titles, including photocopies or your own cover illustrations.

▶ A biography with a photograph of the writer.

▶ A copy of any letters you write and any replies you receive. Your letters may be asking for information or commenting on the books you have read.

▶ Your own blurb for at least one of the books alongside the publisher's blurb.

▶ An interview with a character. Make sure this gives a clear indication of the character's personality and how he/she deals with the problems in the story.

▶ An alternative ending to one of the books or an extra chapter adding to the story. Explain, as a note at the end, why you think your new version or chapter is an improvement on the original.

▶ Short accounts of why you would recommend any of these books to teenage readers. Don't give away the plot and avoid simply retelling the story here.

▶ Illustration of characters or scenes with relevant quotations.

▶ Time-chart of events in one or more of the books.

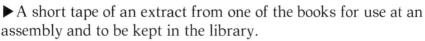 ▶ A short tape of an extract from one of the books for use at an assembly and to be kept in the library.

FUTURES

DECISION-MAKING AND SIMULATIONS

In this unit you will be thinking about the future. You will be selecting the contents of a time capsule, describing everyday objects to people from another planet, working on a simulation in which you choose a delegation of earth people for a Peace Mission in the year 2050, and writing about *your* vision of the future.

When a space-probe is sent out into outer space a time-capsule is sometimes put together. This is a container filled with objects or descriptions of some aspects of our society that are typical of the time we live in. These might be books, pictures, tapes, videos, films, or any significant object. The container is sealed and sent into space. If it is discovered it is supposed to give a clear idea of the way of life of the people it represents.

In pairs, imagine that you are putting together a time-capsule for this year and are trying to represent life on earth as you experience it.

Choose ten items to include in the capsule and write a clear description of why you have chosen each item. Remember that the reasons why you chose an item are more important than the item itself. You might like to draw them and present your capsule as a labelled diagram. The diagram below might help you.

A Martian Sends a Post-Card Home

Caxtons are mechanical birds with many wings
and some are treasured for their markings —

they cause the eyes to melt
or the body to shriek without pain.

I have never seen one fly, but
sometimes they perch on the hand.

Mist is when the sky is tired of flight
and rests its soft machine on ground:

then the world is dim and bookish
like engravings under tissue paper.

Rain is when the earth is television.
It has the property of making colours darker.

Model T is a room with the lock inside —
a key is turned to free the world

for movement, so quick there is a film
to watch for anything missed.

But time is tied to the wrist
or kept in a box, ticking with impatience.

In homes, a haunted apparatus sleeps,
that snores when you pick it up.

If the ghost cries, they carry it
to their lips and soothe it to sleep

with sounds. And yet, they wake it up
deliberately, by tickling with a finger.

Only the young are allowed to suffer
openly. Adults go to a punishment room

with water but nothing to eat.
They lock the door and suffer the noises

alone. No one is exempt
and everyone's pain has a different smell.

At night, when all the colours die,
they hide in pairs

and read about themselves —
in colour, with their eyelids shut.

Craig Raine

When you read this poem you need to imagine that a Martian on holiday on earth is sending home information about this strange planet. Different things are described in the poem. Some are fairly clear descriptions, others are not so easy.

Work in pairs and see if you can discover what is being described and how each part of the description fits the object. You need to give yourselves a time-limit then compare your guesses with other pairs.

Here are some clues to help you understand the poem.
▶ William Caxton was one of the first people to invent a printing machine. Before that all books had to be copied out by hand.
▶ The Ford Motor Company produced a car called the Model T. It was one of the first mass-produced cars. Use of driving mirrors is an important part of driving.
▶ Other parts of the poem deal with natural things like rain and mist, or manufactured things like telephones, watches, and toilets. You must work out the final four lines for yourself.

Now imagine you are a space-traveller from another planet coming to earth for the first time. How would you describe the following everyday objects or organisations or people? Choose some of your own if you like. When you have worked out some ideas try to link them as a poem in the same way that Craig Raine did.

washing machine	flower	iron
umbrella	bicycle	supermarket
shower	high rise block of flats	bus
bikini	submarine	swimming-pool
teacher	toaster	TV set
police-station	snow	baby
church	book	telephone
electric fire	cat	telegraph pole.

The Peace Mission

The second part of this unit is about the preparation for a meeting in the future between a delegation of visitors from outer space and a group representing earth-people.

Anybody who tries to write about the future will have to work out what kind of a world there will be. The scenario might be optimistic or pessimistic. Technology may have made life easy or science may have destroyed the planet, wars might be tearing the world apart or people might have learned to live in peace. For the purposes of this simulation it is assumed that the world is much the same as it is now except that people have learned to live in harmony, the centres of power are shared among the continents, space travel is commonplace, and regular contact is made with intelligent beings from outer space. Here in Britain we have a multiracial society where people generally get on well with each other.

This is how the people in Britain first hear the news of the peace mission.

It has been announced from the 2050 United Nations Convention in Lima that for the first time a delegation of visitors from outer space is to meet in the Autumn at the Peace Mission in Lusaka. The Delegation has asked that each earth nation should send four representatives to meet them. Their intention is to share ideas about the culture of each nation in an attempt to bring about greater peace and understanding both on earth and between the galaxies. All translations will be done at the same time by the Inter Galactic Voice Syntax Scrambler.

The Minister for Peace and Understanding said in Newcastle today that the search was now on to find four suitable British representatives. Local Authorities have been instructed in the methods they should use to select the candidates.

Selecting the British Delegation

The British Selection Committee has drawn up a short-list from the thousands of applicants. Only four of these can be chosen.

Your group should now read through the following profiles of the six short-listed candidates.

Robert Hamilton

Robert is twenty and lives at:
    Hut 4,
    Sevenoaks Disaster Aid Force Barracks,
    Kent.

Robert is a commando in the British Disaster Aid Force. His grandparents came to live in England from Barbados in the West Indies in the 1970s. After a period of unemployment, Robert joined the aid force and did a two-year tour of duty with the United Nations. There he was commended for his bravery. Following intensive training Robert was accepted for recruitment to the BAS (British Air Service). He has extraordinary physical endurance and is an expert in the technology of survival. Robert is loyal, always obeys commands and supports his superiors. Robert never smokes and rarely drinks alcohol. He has a collection of over 3,000 antique toy soldiers and is the drummer in the Sevenoaks Barracks rock band but he is also interested in opera.

Sally Hughes

Sally Hughes is twenty-six years old and lives at:
    The Old Mill,
    Bandford,
    Devon.

Sally is the daughter of a Cabinet Minister. She left school at sixteen without taking any exams. She then formed her own dance group which was generally considered to be the most adventurous and interesting in Britain. She divides her time between her small farm in Devon and Covent Garden. She is their youngest ever dance director.

   She has a very strong personality and can be difficult to work with but always brings out the best in talented people. She is a vegetarian and supports animal rights.

Indira Kapur

Professor Indira is forty-five years old and lives at:
    30, Alcroft Rd.,
    Swansea,
    Wales.

The daughter of a Bengali greengrocer, Professor Kapur was born in the East End of London. She attended Garth Green Comprehensive School and won a scholarship to Oxford University. She obtained a first-class B.Sc. degree. Her speciality is developing crops which can thrive in difficult conditions.

Some years ago Professor Kapur led a small expedition up the Amazon and lived with Indian tribes there. She was very successful, first in establishing herself as their friend and then in improving their health by introducing new crops. As a result she was honoured by the Brazilian Congress. She is currently working as a lecturer at the Polytechnic of Swansea.

Professor Indira does not drink alcohol but is a heavy smoker. She is an active member of the Swansea Amateur Dramatic Society.

Nikos Karavias

Nikos is thirty-seven years old and lives at:
    4 Fenton Avenue,
    Aberdeen,
    Scotland.

Nikos Karavias is disabled and looks after the home while his wife works. They have two children. At school he got five GCSEs with a high grade in Human Biology and is a trained dental technician.

Two years ago Nikos was paralysed from the waist down in a car crash. He has been confined to a wheelchair ever since. However, Nikos has not allowed his disability to ruin his life. In his spare time he works for a local hospital, raising money and doing office work. Nikos has set up a national organisation to help the newly disabled adjust to their new lives.

He does not smoke and recently took part in the British Paraplegic Sports Week representing Scotland at table tennis.

Jenny Knight

Jenny Knight is fifty-five years old and lives at:
    12, Baker St,
    Marylebone,
    London.

Jenny Knight is a company director and a millionaire twice over. She built up her business single-handed having taken over a small bankrupt firm. She sacked inefficient workers and soon made the firm profitable. Jenny never gives to charity because, she says, her companies give work to thousands of people and that is charity enough. She is a healthy and active fifty-five-year-old who often works a twelve-hour day. It is not generally known that Jenny Knight spends a considerable amount of time as a prison visitor and employs ex-prisoners whenever possible.

Alfred Sing

Alfred Sing is sixty-four and lives at:
    The Woodlands,
    4 Red Hill,
    Newcastle on Tyne.

Alfred is a nuclear physicist working for the Ministry of Energy. He is one of the world's leading experts on the medical treatment for the effects of radiation. Alfred came to this country as a child from Hong Kong in the 1990s. He is an expert chess player and is well known as a presenter of popular science programmes on TV.

The application form

Printed on the following page is the application form which each of the applicants had to complete. Choose any one of the short-listed candidates and fill in a form *for that person* using the details you have been given. If you work in groups of six you could each choose a different candidate.

Write a paragraph in which you state three or four reasons why you think your chosen person should be selected as a British Delegate on the Peace Mission.

```
Name _____ Age, Sex _____
Address _____
_____
Occupation _____
Current place of work _____
Educational experience _____
Interests _____
Disabilities _____
```

Drawing up the questions

Imagine your group is the panel interviewing the short-listed candidates. Work out ten questions to ask each candidate. The questions should be framed to bring out the best in each person and to give each one the opportunity to talk at length.

Closed questions are ones which do not help a candidate to say much more than 'yes' or 'no', or to give a short fact which is already known. For example: *How old are you?* — a bad question because you already know the answer.

Open questions are ones which provide opportunities to give opinions, talk about experiences, and explain reasons or feelings. For example: *What have you been doing in the last five years?* — a good question because each candidate has the same opportunity to respond well.

The interview

The interview can be organised in different ways:
▶ Select six of the class to act out the roles of the short-listed candidates. The rest of the class will act as the interviewing panel with the teacher as chairperson. Before the interview the panel must decide on the ten best questions.
▶ The class can divide into groups of ten with six candidates and four members of the interviewing panel.
▶ Work in pairs taking turns to be candidate or interviewer.
Whichever method you use you must make notes as you go along for use in the final stage, Decision time.

Decision time

The selection committee must come to a decision about the four candidates who, taken together, will give the truest picture of our society. Your group task now is to *write the report* that goes to the Minister of Peace and Understanding explaining the reason why these four have been chosen as delegates.

A story set in the future

The final part of this unit is to write a story about life in the future. This gives you a chance to look at our society as it is today and to speculate on how it is developing.

First of all set out the limits of your story, e.g.
▶ it will be set on this planet
▶ there will be a human society of some sort
▶ there will be two or three characters who have a story line.

Secondly, decide what changes will have taken place. Is your story going to be a warning about how badly wrong things might go? Or will it be an ideal picture of how good life might be if we get rid of such things as hunger, disease, violence, poverty, and war.

Thirdly, decide how far into the future your story will be set
▶ within your probable lifetime, e.g. fifty years ahead
▶ 100 years ahead
▶ more than 100 years.

Here are two possible scenarios to show the kind of outline you should make before you start your story.

(a) This story is a bleak warning to the reader about what might happen if we are not careful. It is set fifty years from now in England. Practically all work is done by automation and everyone has as much free time as they want. The cities have spread out as the population has increased and it is very difficult to get away from the stress of living in a small, cramped flat. Nearly everyone is bored and most people are scared because of the gangs of youths that nobody can control. Peter and Joan are two seventeen-year-olds who live in what used to be called Nottingham in the centre of England. They are dissatisfied with their lives so they decide to go to the seaside which they have only ever seen on films. They have the idea that if only they can live near the sea they will be able to get back to a more natural way of life. This story is about how they make the journey only to find the sea a stinking, polluted oil-slick where nothing lives.

(b) It is 100 years from now. People have plenty of leisure time but they know how to use it. The population has decreased rather than increased and there is plenty of opportunity for travel around England's beautiful countryside. This story concerns Peter and Joan who are on a journey going back to Liverpool where their grandparents were born. They have only known this happy society so they are most interested to meet an old man who joins them on their journey and who starts to tell them of his experiences of over eighty years before.

LIFE STORY

AUTOBIOGRAPHY

How to start

Up till now in your school career, it may be that most of the pieces of writing that you've done will have been fairly short. Writing something longer takes more planning and, of course, more time.

One of the main problems of doing a long piece of writing is knowing what to write about, and how to keep it going. The main fear is that you'll run out of things to say. The best subject to choose, then, is one you know a lot about, and if the subject is yourself, and your own life, then you know more about that than anyone else. You're the world expert!

But the writing still has to be organised, so as not to go on too long, or finish too soon, or repeat itself. In this unit there are some examples of good autobiographical writing, with some practice activities for you to do after reading them, followed by ten suggestions to bear in mind when you begin a full-length piece of work.

You may think you're too young to write your own life story. After all, most of the world's famous autobiographies have been written by people in their old age. But the fourth and fifth years of secondary school are a turning-point in some ways, because after it you tend to be treated more and more as a young adult, and your memories of your childhood, and how you felt, will tend to fade.

 The extracts in this unit are there to give ideas for your own talking and writing, but they all contain interesting points that you may want to discuss before bringing in your own experiences.

Early years and memories

I don't think it's good enough for me to say that I was born in the Gorbals, in May, 1944, and leave it at that. Perhaps it's all I can say, but who am I? I don't really know who I am. The one thing I am certain of is the womb I came from. And if it were possible for one to choose the womb that one was conceived in, then this is the one I'd have chosen. My Mother, Bessie, was in many ways too good for this world, and the more I got to know the world the more I believed this.

When I was born my Mother already had two sons, Tommy and Pat — aged four and eight respectively. My father's name was Tommy. From birth to the age of five my memories are vague snatches of a complete family living in a room-and-kitchen in an old Gorbals tenement building. Throughout this period certain memories remained with me that were connected with the physical and spiritual feeling of the house, such as the big coal fire that was always burning in the kitchen, which was a very small room though it managed to hold the table where everyone ate; the cooker, some furniture, and my parents' bed which sat in a recess. The kitchen was where most things were done, and everyone would sit around the fireplace talking. The fireplace played a principal role in our home as it did in most homes in the district. My father would stand in front of it with his hands behind his back, and this is one of the few memories I have of him. On a Saturday night my mother would get the tin bath out from under the bed and fill it with water to bathe all three of us, one after the other. This was a time I always disliked. Saturday was also the night that my parents' friends and relatives would come up to our house with 'carry-outs' to drink and have a party.

We would be put to bed in the small room while the adults sang songs and danced, but once they started getting mellow with the booze we would get out of bed and mix with them, asking them for money while they were in this happy frame of mind. Parties and people being what they are they would either finish in a fight, or with everyone embracing each other.

The room of our house was where we three boys slept. There was a fireplace in the room but it was rarely used as we couldn't afford it; there were also other pieces of furniture, including a large wardrobe that held the whole family's clothes. Our bed was in a recess with Pat and Tommy sleeping at the top of it and me at their feet to give us more room. I think sleeping with Pat was a good preparation for the tough life ahead because he was the worst sleeper in the world. All through the night he would nip me with his fingers if I moved near his part of the bed, and he would do this instinctively at the slightest infringement onto his area. Other times he would kick, and being the youngest, I had to accept it, though at the time I always resented it and wanted a bed of my own.

Sunday morning was always the essence of family life in our house as Mother would get us all up and made ready for chapel which was at the corner of our road, Sandyfaulds Street. Mother took us all down, giving us a ha'penny each for the collection plate. Leaving chapel was a great occasion as everyone used to eye everyone else up to see what they were wearing, and to see who was there. If anyone had a new suit or new clothes of some kind then they always wore them to chapel. People stopped and talked in the street after mass to gossip, and there was a very close community feeling at such times. From there, Pat, my eldest brother, was sent to the nearby newsagents to buy the Sunday newspapers — no *News of the World* permitted. Mother, Tommy and I returned to the house where she began the breakfast. The Sunday breakfast surpassed all others, as it was ham, eggs, black pudding and potato scones.

Jimmy Boyle

▶ Where and when were you born?

▶ What are your very earliest memories? Most people can't remember much that happened before they were about four.

▶ What were the adults, and the older brothers and sisters (if any), in your life like?

▶ What events stand out most clearly in the first five or six years?

Feelings, hopes, beliefs

When Richard Wright was very young, he had some strange ideas in his head. Years later, he made this list of them in his autobiography.

If I pulled a hair from a horse's tail and sealed it in a jar of my own urine, the hair would turn overnight into a snake.

If I passed a Catholic sister or mother dressed in black and smiled and I allowed her to see my teeth, I would surely die.

If I walked under a leaning ladder, I would certainly have bad luck.

If I kissed my elbow, I would turn into a girl.

If my right ear itched, then something good was being said about me by somebody.

If I touched a hunchback's hump, then I would never be sick.

If I placed a safety pin on a steel railroad track and let a train run over it, the safety pin would turn into a pair of bright brand-new scissors.

If I heard a voice and no human being was near, then either God or the Devil was trying to talk to me.

If my nose itched, somebody was going to visit me.

If I mocked a crippled man, then God would make me crippled.

If I used the name of God in vain, then God would strike me dead.

If it rained while the sun was shining, then the Devil was beating his wife.

If the stars twinkled more than usual on any given night, it meant that the angels in heaven were happy and were flitting across the floors of heaven; and since stars were merely holes ventilating heaven, the twinkling came from the angels flitting past the hole that admitted air into the holy home of God.

If I broke a mirror, I would have seven years of bad luck.

If I was good to my mother, I would grow old and rich.

If I had a cold and tied a worn, dirty sock about my throat before I went to bed, the cold would be gone the next morning.

If I looked at the sun through a piece of smoked glass on Easter Sunday morning, I would see the sun shouting in praise of a Risen Lord.

If a man confessed anything on his deathbed, it was the truth: no man could stare death in the face and lie.

If you spat on each grain of corn that was planted, the corn would grow tall and bear well.

If I spilt salt, I should toss a pinch over my left shoulder to ward off misfortune.

If I covered a mirror when a storm was raging, the lightning would not strike me.

If I stepped over a broom that was lying on the floor, I would have bad luck.

If I walked in my sleep, then God was trying to lead me somewhere to do a good deed for Him.

Richard Wright

▶ Make a list of any beliefs like these that you had when you were very young.

▶ Can you remember stories, songs and games from the streets or the playground? Write about those that you can recall.

▶ Were there things that you just couldn't understand? Explain them now that you are older.

Off to school

Carl Jung wrote his autobiography when he was eighty-three, but he never forgot something that happened to him one day when he was twelve.

My twelfth year was indeed a fateful one for me. One day in the early summer of 1887 I was standing in the cathedral square, waiting for a classmate who went home by the same route as myself. It was twelve o'clock, and the morning classes were over. Suddenly another boy gave me a shove that knocked me off my feet. I fell, striking my head against the kerbstone so hard that I almost lost consciousness. For about half an hour afterwards I was a little dazed. At the moment I felt the blow the thought flashed through my mind: 'Now you won't have to go to school any more.' I was only half unconscious, but I remained lying there a few moments longer than was strictly necessary, chiefly in order to avenge myself on my assailant. Then people picked me up and took me to a house nearby, where two elderly spinster aunts lived.

From then on I began to have fainting spells whenever I had to return to school, and whenever my parents set me to doing my homework. For more than six months I stayed away from school, and for me that was a picnic. I was free, could dream for hours, be anywhere I liked, in the woods or by the water, or draw. I resumed my battle pictures and furious scenes of war, of old castles that were being assaulted or burned, or drew page upon page of caricatures. Similar caricatures sometimes appear to me before falling asleep to this day, grinning masks that constantly move and change, among them familiar faces of people who soon afterwards died.

Carl Jung

▶ Are your first memories of school good ones or bad ones?
▶ Which activities did you enjoy?
▶ Would you have preferred to stay at home?

In his autobiography, Richard Wright has actually reconstructed his first day at school in detail, even giving the words that were spoken. Can you remember things that were said several years ago?

The first half of the school day passed without incident. I sat looking at the strange reading books, following the lessons. The subjects seemed simple and I felt that I could keep up. My anxiety was still in me; I was wondering how I would get on with the boys. Each new school meant a new area of life to be conquered. Were the boys tough? How hard did they fight? I took it for granted that they fought.

At noon recess I went into the school grounds and a group of boys sauntered up to me, looked at me from my head to my feet, whispering among themselves. I leaned against a wall, trying to conceal my uneasiness.

'Where you from?' a boy asked abruptly.

'Jackson,' I answered.

'How come they make you people so ugly in Jackson?' he demanded.

There was loud laughter.

'You're not any too good-looking yourself,' I countered instantly.

'Oh!'

'Aw!'

'You hear what he told 'im?'

'You think you're smart, don't you?' the boy asked, sneering.

'Listen, I ain't picking a fight,' I said. 'But if you want to fight, I'll fight.'

'Hunh, hard guy, ain't you?'

'As hard as you.'

'Do you know who you can tell that to?' he asked me.

'And you know who you can tell it back to?' I asked.

'Are you talking about my mama?' he asked, edging forward.

'If you want it that way,' I said.

This was my test. If I failed now, I would have failed at school, for the first trial came not in books, but in how one's fellows took one, what value they placed upon one's willingness to fight.

'Take back what you said,' the boy challenged me.

'Make me,' I said.

The crowd howled, sensing a fight. The boy hesitated, weighing his chances of beating me.

'You ain't gonna take what that new boy said, is you?' someone taunted the boy.

The boy came close. I stood my ground. Our faces were four inches apart.

'You think I'm scared of you, don't you?' he asked.

'I told you what I think,' I said.

Somebody, eager and afraid we would not fight, pushed the boy and he bumped into me. I shoved him away violently.

'Don't push me!' the boy said.

'Then keep off me!' I said.

He was pushed again and I struck out with my right and caught him in the mouth. The crowd yelled, milled, surging so close that I could barely lift my arm to land a blow. When either of us tried to strike the other, we would be thrown off balance by the screaming boys. Every blow landed elicited shouts of delight. Knowing that if I did not win or make a good showing I would have to fight a new boy each day, I fought tigerishly, trying to leave a scar, seeking to draw blood as proof that I was not a coward, that I could take care of myself. The bell rang and the crowd pulled us apart. The fight seemed a draw.

'I ain't through with you!' the boy shouted.

'Go to hell!' I answered.

In the classroom the boys asked me questions about myself; I was someone worth knowing. When the bell rang for school to be dismissed, I was set to fight again; but the boy was not in sight.

On my way home I found a cheap ring in the streets and at once I knew what I was going to do with it. The ring had a red stone held by tiny prongs which I loosened, took the stone out, leaving the sharp tiny prongs jutting up. I slid the ring on to my finger and shadow boxed. Now, by God, let a goddam bully come and I would show him how to fight; I would leave a crimson streak on his face with every blow.

But I never had to use the ring. After I had exhibited my new weapon at school, a description of it spread among the boys. I challenged my enemy to another fight, but he would not respond. Fighting was not now necessary. I had been accepted.

Richard Wright

Living space

The place, or places, where you've lived are an important part of your autobiography. Here Bonnie Benjamin, aged sixteen, looks back on moving house from one part of North London to another. She manages to write about some difficult times with a sense of humour.

Our house in Petherton Road was slowly beginning to decay and was subsequently visited by a health inspector, a tall pale-looking man who poked and sniffed at the walls and ceilings and then declared our house to be dangerous. He said that it was a fire-hazard, a health hazard, and generally unfit for human habitation. He left looking somewhat shocked that we were all quite healthy and happy and managed to live in relative comfort, when the house was practically caving in on us. The whole side of the house, facing the garden, was gradually collapsing due to some kind of fungi growing on the inside of the house. So the whole side of the house had to be supported by scaffold. Even when me and my family came back from a day out and found that our ceiling had collapsed, because of the dampness, no one bothered to panic since it had already happened to everyone else in the house. We all huddled into the sitting room where we spent a few warm and cosy nights on mattresses until the ceiling was repaired.

Anyway, the day soon came when the health visitor's report was noticed by the landlord and we had to move away family by family. The Oyedeles upstairs moved first and seemed to take days and nights about it too. They refused to rent a van and so moved all their furniture piece by piece in their

little red car. For weeks we would hear the creeping up and down the stairs in the middle of the night, moving furniture and having little whispered arguments in their own confusing language. They never did tell us where they went so we never saw them again.

The day soon came for my family to move and it took us a whole week to get everything ready and packed into huge tea-chests. I never realised one family could possess so many things in such a small habitation and so I began to make a vague check and investigate further, all the things I had never seen before. It was quite exciting, moving, the things one managed to discover under one's bed, apart from spiders, was unbelievable! The day we moved was a bright, but cold day in October. My Mum had painted such a beautiful picture of our new flat that the sadness we all felt to be leaving our friends behind was made more bearable.

'We gonna have our own toilet,' I told my friends.

'Cor!' they all exclaimed, to my delight.

'An' our own bathroom,' my sister Barbara stated.

'Your own bathroom?' my friends repeated.

'An' our own front door,' Beverley finished.

'Your *own* front door!' said my friends, and then they shook their heads in disbelief.

Still, on the day the removal van came, the Sempers, the Dyers, and the Frances all watched us with envy as we loaded our furniture into it and happily waved goodbye.

211 Morris House, on the other side of Islington was a castle compared to our old flat. We had four rooms, not including the kitchen, the toilet, the bathroom and, of course, our own front door!

I was nine at the time and my sisters and I all found the flat to be absolute luxury at first. But then when the crunch came and we had to start making new friends all over again we began to wish we had never moved out of that crumbling old house away from all that had been familiar to us. We soon learnt the hard way that estate kids were not the same as kids who lived on nice little streets in nice big houses. They made it quite plain to me and my sisters that they didn't appreciate us 'wogs' moving into the flat that one of their friends had just left. So we were pushed off the swings until we realised that a taste of their own medicine soon provided an effective cure.

It was not until we had spent the half-term holiday settling down and getting the gist of things, when my sisters and I were faced with the realisation of having to start a new school. It was all too much for me so I spent my last days writing letters to my lost friends in Petherton Road, reminiscing on the 'good old days'.

 What are the important places in *your* life?

A full autobiography

 If you've done the four pieces of writing in this unit, you're well on your way to an autobiography. Here are some more headings that would make it more complete:

▶ My Family
▶ Friends and Enemies
▶ Important Events
▶ Secondary School
▶ Likes and Dislikes
▶ Hopes for the Future

You can arrange all the pieces you've done in roughly chronological order.

If you prefer to write an autobiography as a story that moves from year to year, you'll need to make notes about the main points that will go into each year.

For practice, take any one year in your life and jot down the memories that come to mind. You'll be surprised how one memory can call up another, and another . . .

Advice on autobiography writing

1. Don't try and write this all at once. It should be spread out over a number of weeks.
2. Let your teacher or a friend read sections when you've finished them, and get their comments.
3. Don't put anything in that might embarrass you or your family, or which is better left private. After all, you don't know who may read it.
4. Ask parents and relatives to help. They may be delighted to join in the writing task, especially about things you were too young to know.
5. Read what others in your class are writing. It will give you ideas.
6. If you get stuck, ask your teacher for advice.
7. Include maps, drawings, and photographs if you need to.
8. This autobiography may be the longest and most ambitious writing you've ever done, or ever will do. Put a cover on it, get it photocopied if you can, and keep it. You'll find it interesting to read in a few years from now.

Macbeth may be the first play by Shakespeare that you have read. If so, you have chosen a good place to start, because *Macbeth* is probably his most gripping play. It has been performed on stage regularly for at least three hundred years; it has been made into a film several times, even in Japan; it has been shown on television and made the basis for modern plays.

Set in Scotland, it is the story of a nobleman who, under the influence of three 'weird sisters', commits a series of terrible murders (encouraged by his wife) and in the end pays the price for his crimes. Shakespeare called the play *a tragedy*, meaning that it shows the downfall of a great man and is meant to make an audience feel both fear and pity as they watch it.

Shakespeare wrote his plays to be performed on the stage. He does not seem to have taken much trouble over preserving his scripts, probably because he never imagined that one day people would sit down and read them. The best way to experience *Macbeth* is to see it performed.

In this section are suggestions for work on *Macbeth* aimed at increasing your understanding of the play. All of them involve discussing aspects of the play in groups, and many of them have suggestions for writing that could be included in a Literature folder.

The text referred to in this book is the *Signet Shakespeare*. Each quotation or reference is identified by Act, Scene, and Line, so that Act I, Scene iii, Line 47 is printed: I. iii. 47.

Public . . . and private

Look like the innocent flower
but be the serpent under it . . . (I. v. 64)

This is Lady Macbeth's advice to Macbeth as they prepare to welcome King Duncan to their castle. Already the king has been deceived by someone he trusted, and he has observed that a person's *public* face does not necessarily reveal their *private* thoughts.

There's no art
To find the mind's construction in the face:
He was a gentleman on whom I built
An absolute trust.
(I.iv.12)

This idea that 'things are not what they seem' reappears again and
again in *Macbeth*:
▶ The witches' prophecy *seems* to be good but is really bad.
▶ Macbeth's castle *seems* to be safe but is really a place of murder.
▶ What *seems* to be a wood is really an army.

Of course once the plan to murder Duncan takes root, Macbeth and
Lady Macbeth have to live the rest of their lives with a public face of
innocence and a private feeling of guilt.

Here are some quotations from the play which express the
difference between the public face (what seems to be) and the private
thoughts (what really is):

False face must hide what the false heart doth know (I.vii.83)

To show an unfelt sorrow is an office
Which the false man does easy. (II.iii.138)

. . . but wail his fall
Who I myself struck down. (III.i.122)

Gentle my lord, sleek o'er your rugged looks,
Be bright and jovial among your guests tonight. (III.ii.28)

And make our faces vizards to our hearts
Disguising what they are. (III.ii.34)

Your own story

Write a story in which the main character has to:
'Look like the innocent flower, but be the serpent under it.'

It does not have to be a modern version of *Macbeth*, but you could
make the story more interesting by relating it to the play.

(a) You could use the quotations above as chapter or section
headings. For example, the first section, in which the villain
meets the victim and has to act innocent, could have the title:
'False face must hide what the false heart doth know'.

(b) You could base your story on the same structure as the play *Macbeth*:
1. The false welcome
2. The treacherous deed
3. Fake grief
4. Acting the innocent.

Some suggestions:
▶ the star player on the school team —
an accident is arranged by the person who has been kept out of the team . . .
▶ the well-respected leader of the gang (or oil company?) —
a nasty accident is arranged by the person next in line for leadership . . .

Persuasion

Lady Macbeth has to persuade Macbeth to murder the King and so make the weird sisters' prophecy come true.

Can you remember how she does it? Here are some examples of her tactics (from I.vii.35-61):

▶ *Flattery*

> Great Glamis! Worthy Cawdor!
> Greater than both, by the all-hail hereafter.

▶ *Accusing him of cowardice*

> And live a coward in thine own esteem
> Letting 'I dare not' wait upon 'I would'.

▶ *Questioning his manhood*

> When you durst do it, then you were a man.

▶ *Reassuring*

> But screw your courage to the sticking point,
> And we'll not fail.

Your own scene

Write a scene from a play in which one person is persuading another person to do something wrong, for example:
▶ to commit a murder to gain the insurance money
▶ to break into a shop
▶ to cheat in an exam.

This second person had agreed to go along with the idea but has decided to change his or her mind. Their first speech could be a modern version of Macbeth's 'We will proceed no further with this business'.

Try to use all four of the tactics used by Lady Macbeth. Do not worry too much about explaining the story; concentrate on making the persuasion as powerful as possible.

Guilt

A little water clears us of this deed (II. iii. 66)

Lady Macbeth is trying to convince Macbeth that all will be well after they have murdered Duncan. The rest of the play shows us how wrong she is.

Already Macbeth is feeling guilty; his conscience is beginning to work on him. He may be King, but is he safe? Will he be able to live with himself? He is not only guilty, but afraid.

Several things happen to show us how this guilt and fear affect him:
▶ He fears Banquo and has him killed.
▶ He is deeply disturbed at the banquet and 'sees' the ghost of Banquo.
▶ He cannot sleep, and when he does is afflicted by terrible dreams.
▶ He can trust no one; he must murder more and more people in order to feel safe.
▶ He goes back to the witches desperate for more information.

Your own story

Write a story in which guilt and fear work on someone who has committed a crime. Try to include in your story some of the things which happen to Macbeth:
▶ has trouble sleeping; suffers from terrible nightmares
▶ has to commit more crimes to cover his/her tracks
▶ begins to see things
▶ desperately needs reassurance.

You could write this story from the point of view of the guilty person. The story could be in the form of his/her diary or even just that person's thoughts.

Predictions

1. All hail Macbeth! Hail to thee, Thane of Cawdor!
2. All hail Macbeth, that shalt be King hereafter. (I.iii)
3. Macbeth! Beware MacDuff.
4.   Laugh to scorn
   The power of man, for none of woman born
   Shall harm Macbeth.
5. Macbeth shall never vanquished be until
   Great Burnam wood to high Dunsinane Hill
   Shall come against him. (IV.i)

The weird sisters make five different predictions to Macbeth. All of them come true.

Banquo is wary of predictions because he believes that the 'instruments of darkness' tell truths in order to 'betray us in deepest consequence'.

A prediction may appear to be a happy one, but the final consequences may be far from happy.

Your own story

Write a story in which the main character receives several predictions which sound good, but in fact turn out to be very harmful.

The story could begin like this:

It sounded too good to be true when the old fortune teller at the fair made her prediction. Now I wish I had never gone near the tent. She had looked at my hand and said . . .

A trial

The trial of Macbeth and Lady Macbeth

Suppose that Macbeth and Lady Macbeth were arrested after the murder of Duncan. When the case comes to court, Macbeth pleads guilty to the murder, but Lady Macbeth pleads not guilty.

Two lawyers are needed. One, a defence lawyer, will try to get Macbeth a lighter sentence by showing that, although he did the murder, there are things to be said in his favour. The other, a prosecuting lawyer, will try to show that Lady Macbeth deserves a heavy sentence, even though she did not actually kill the King.

Preparing your case

Work in pairs.

1. Decide whether you will defend Macbeth or prosecute Lady Macbeth.
2. Working from memory, find all the arguments you can to support your case. You will need to consider questions like these:

▶ *Macbeth*

(a) What kind of man was he before the murder? (Did he have a good reputation?)
(b) Did anybody put strong pressure on him, and if so, how?
(c) Was he in his right mind? (Any strange experiences, hallucinations, etc.?)
(d) Did he find it easy to murder Duncan?
(e) Did he regret killing Duncan? (Any signs of remorse, or disgust with himself?)

▶ *Lady Macbeth*

(a) Did she suggest murder to her husband?
(b) Did she encourage him to do it?
(c) Did she put pressure on him to do it?
(d) Did she help plan it?
(e) Did she help carry it out?
(f) Did she try to cover it up?
(g) What did she feel about it afterwards?

3. Look back at the play (up to the end of Act II, Scene ii) and find things that Macbeth or Lady Macbeth actually said, which you quote to prove your points, e.g.:

(a) Duncan calls Macbeth 'Valiant cousin! Worthy gentleman!' and promises to make him Thane of Cawdor.

The captain, speaking of the battle, says:

'Brave Macbeth — well he deserves that name.' (I.ii)

(b) When Macbeth says that the King is coming to stay with them that night and leaving the next day, Lady Macbeth says:

'O never
Shall sun that morrow see!'

Later, speaking of murder, she says:

'Leave all the rest to me.' (I.v)

4. Using your notes, write out your speech to the court. Remember that as a lawyer you are allowed to skip over awkward points and just concentrate on the points that suit your case.

Macbeth on the stage

As you work through *Macbeth* for your exam it would be easy to forget that this play was written to be performed on stage.

The person who decides how a play is presented on stage is called the *director*. He or she will read the play very carefully indeed and decide how each scene is going to work on stage. A director will expect the actors to have their own ideas, but he or she will need to have a picture of the whole play.

For each scene of the play a director needs to ask several questions, of which the most important one is:

1. How can I make the audience experience this scene in the way I want them to? (By getting them gripped, laughing, crying, horrified, etc.)

The other questions are:

2. What objects will I have on stage for this scene and where will they be placed?
3. Where will the actors come on to the stage from? Where will they move to, and when? (Actors will be given some freedom in this, but the director must have an overall plan.)
4. How will the actors behave during this scene? What are they supposed to be feeling? How will they show these feelings in the way they move and the way they speak their lines?
5. What will the actors who are not speaking be doing in the background?
6. What will the lighting be like? Will there be any extra sounds? (Music, sound effects, etc.)

Before the director begins rehearsals he/she must visualize the scene in his/her mind's eye and then write notes, usually on a copy of the script. These notes will remind the director of the answers to the questions.

On the next page you will find a page taken from a director's script. You can see she has made notes on the script.

What about stockings over their heads? They must look threatening & cool to begin wilt.

Very dim lighting wilt shadows on the back wall. (perhaps dark clouds).

Scene III. (*Near the palace.*)

First & second come in from E ③ ahead — third is stalking behind.

Enter Three Murderers.

Spoken over his shoulder as he enters.

Stops in mid movement

moves up onto dais

FIRST MURDERER: But who did bid thee join with us?
THIRD MURDERER: Macbeth.
SECOND MURDERER: He needs not our mistrust; since he delivers
     Our offices and what we have to do
     To the direction just.°

This surprises the other two — they both stop.

FIRST MURDERER: Then stand with us.
     The west yet glimmers with some streaks of day.
     Now spurs the lated° traveler apace
     To gain the timely inn [and near approaches
     The subject of our watch.]

We must feel that they are dealing wilt their suspicions.

THIRD MURDERER: Hark! I hear horses.
BANQUO (*Within*): Give us a light there, ho!
SECOND MURDERER: Then 'tis he
FIRST MURDERER: His horses go about.
THIRD MURDERER: Almost a mile: but he does usually —
     So all men do — from hence to th' palace gate
     Make it their walk.

Moves into darkness of E Ⓑ

Flattens himself against back wall.

crouches below dais

Enter Banquo and Fleance, with a torch.

From Ent A with bright single light

1st M follows them round and silently moves onto dais

SECOND MURDERER: A light, a light!
THIRD MURDERER: 'Tis he.
FIRST MURDERER:
BANQUO: It will be rain tonight.
FIRST MURDERER: Let it come down.

Stand to 't. *at Z*

Jumps down
LIGHTS DOWN

Moves centre stage — and B. thrashes about wilt 3 murderers flaying about — B. killed — dropped over dais.

(*They set upon Banquo.*)

BANQUO: O, treachery! Fly, good Fleance, fly, fly, fly!

(*Exit Fleance.*)

Tries Ex B, then makes it back to Ex A

     Thou mayst revenge. O slave! (*Dies.*)
THIRD MURDERER: Who did strike out the light?
FIRST MURDERER: Was 't not the way?°
THIRD MURDERER: There's but one down; the son is fled.
SECOND MURDERER: We have lost best half of our affair.
FIRST MURDERER: Well, let's away and say how much is
     done.   *Exeunt.*

Sits down on the dais exhausted

Here is a plan of the theatre.

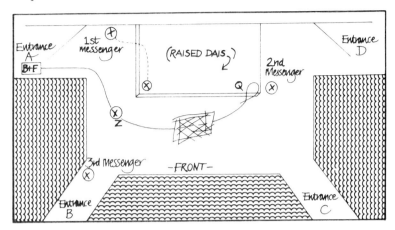

Directing a scene

Here is a list of three scenes in *Macbeth* which a director would need to think about carefully:

Act II, Scene iii, Lines 51 to 125.
The discovery of Duncan's murder and Macbeth and Lady Macbeth's cover-up.
Act III, Scene iv.
The banquet scene in which Macbeth 'sees' the ghost of Banquo.
(N.B. an important decision is whether or not to have Banquo's 'ghost' on stage.)
Act V, Scene i.
The sleep-walking scene.

1. Ask your teacher to photocopy the scene you are interested in directing.
2. Stick your copy of the scene onto a larger sheet of paper so that you have plenty of room to scribble notes.
3. Go through the six questions and decide how you will present the play.
4. You can *either* use the plan of the theatre on this page *or* do a plan of the theatre space in your own school.
5. You will need to include sketches and diagrams to explain the more complicated bits.

Obviously the best way to see how successful you have been as a director is to *try it out* with a group of people in a space. If your ideas work, you might want to go on and put the scene on in front of an audience.

Interviewing the characters

Suppose you had the opportunity to interview some of the characters in *Macbeth*.

▶ Which character would you choose to interview?

▶ What questions would you ask him or her?

Here is part of an interview with Banquo:

INTERVIEWER: Tell me, Banquo, what was your reaction to the witches? Were you scared of them?

BANQUO: Not really. I have seen many strange things in my time, and I don't pretend to understand everything. As I said to Macbeth at the time, 'The earth hath bubbles, as the water has,
And these are of them.'
I was more fascinated than frightened. You must remember that we were on our way back from the battle. I was exhausted. I couldn't make them out, but I was suspicious.

INTERVIEWER: And what about Macbeth? How do you think he reacted?

BANQUO: He was very jumpy from the start. When they made their prophecies, I was surprised to see him become very upset, because all the predictions favoured him.

INTERVIEWER: Why was he upset?

BANQUO: I'm not sure. We'd both been given some good news, even if it was conflicting. Then when one of the prophecies came true almost immediately, I was a bit shaken . . .

Some suggestions

Here is a list of characters it might be interesting to interview:
▶ Macbeth: You could interview Macbeth at different times during the play or interview him just before the battle and ask him about whether he has any regrets.
▶ Lady Macbeth: Ask her about how she planned the murder, and what were the problems. Ask her about her impression of Macbeth before the murder of Duncan, and then after.
▶ Banquo: Get him to talk about his suspicions of Macbeth.
▶ The Doctor: What was life like in the castle in the later stages? How did he feel after he had seen Lady Macbeth sleep walk?

When you write your interview try to include lines from the play (look back at the sample interview with Banquo for some ideas).

Macbeth: hero or villain?

To help you write an essay about Macbeth, which explores his role in the play:

1. Discuss with someone whether each of these statements is true.
   (a) Macbeth is a brave and loyal soldier.
   (b) Macbeth is a fool to believe what the witches say.
   (c) Macbeth is weak compared to Lady Macbeth.
   (d) Macbeth regrets killing Duncan.
   (e) Although Banquo's ghost terrifies him, Macbeth doesn't regret killing Banquo.
   (f) Macbeth rules Scotland by murder and terror.
   (g) Macbeth admits to himself he is evil, so he is honest, and not a hypocrite.
   (h) Macbeth never loses his bravery, even when he realises the witches have tricked him.

Appearance and reality

Macbeth is full of things that are not what they seem to be, and people whose *reality* is different from their *appearance*.

Here are some examples:
1. The weird sisters look like men *and* women. (I.iii.46)
2. It's not certain at first whether they really exist, or are just visions. (I.iii.82)
3. Macbeth and Lady Macbeth seem to Duncan to be loyal, loving and trustworthy, when he enters their castle.
4. Banquo describes the castle where Duncan is to die as a pleasant and healthy place.
5. Macbeth and Lady Macbeth *seem* horrified at Duncan's murder.

Your own examples

There are many examples of this kind in the play. Can you continue the list in the same way?

Here are some hints to help you find the examples. In your list mark which is which with an A or a B.

a dagger	two guilty grooms	false promises
a ghost	a wood	a wicked prince
a 'foul and fair' day		

A. Sometimes we, the audience, know that the appearance is different from the reality before some of the characters.
B. Sometimes we are in the dark just like them, and discover later what the truth is.

Darkness . . .

The work on this and the following page is to help you look more closely at the way Shakespeare's language affects an audience as much as the events in the play.

1. *Macbeth* was first performed indoors, in front of a small audience.
2. In Shakespeare's time there was, of course, no electric light; the play-room would have been lit by candles. If you've ever been in a place lit only by candles, you'll know that they give bright spots of light, and deep shadows that move as people move past the candles. (Candlelight also affects the way faces appear — half in light, half in shadow.)
3. You remember that some of the most important events in *Macbeth* take place in darkness: the murder of Duncan, the murder of Banquo, Macbeth's visit to the witches, and Lady Macbeth's sleep-walking. Shakespeare chose to do this deliberately — it's not hard to think why.
4. Many of the characters mention darkness as the play goes on. The repetition of word-images of dark and night feeds our imaginations, so that we never forget for long, even while reading the play in broad daylight, that darkness hangs over the play. Here are some examples:

(Macbeth thinking about killing Duncan — I.v.50)

> Come, thick night,
> And pall thee in the dimmest smoke of hell,
> That my keen knife see not the wound it makes,
> Nor heaven peep through the blanket of the dark,
> To cry 'Hold, hold!'

Banquo, just before the murder — II.i.5)

> There's husbandry in heaven.
> Their candles are all out.'

5. Shakespeare also gives us word-pictures of darkness *struggling* with light, and darkness winning. When this is repeated, it creates

a feeling, or *atmosphere* in the play which we can remember even when we have forgotten the words themselves.
(Macbeth thinking about killing Duncan — I.iv.50)

> Stars, hide your fires.
> Let not light see my black and deep desires.

Talk about these images together. Do you understand what they mean? For example, what does 'dark night strangles the travelling lamp' mean? What do the words 'Light thickens' mean to you?

When you have discussed them, copy out each quotation and write notes on the meanings you arrive at in your discussion.

. . . and disease

There is another chain of images in the play which deal this time with disease. They create an atmosphere in which Scotland is like a healthy body which contains a deadly disease — Macbeth — waiting to break out. These are the references for the images:

I.iii.23	Who is causing this sickness?
II.ii.45	Why does Lady Macbeth tell Macbeth his brain is sick?
III.iv.87	Why does Macbeth lie like this?
IV.iii.214	How is Macduff's revenge like a medicine?
V.ii.62	Why is this disease beyond the Doctor to cure?
V.ii.26	How will Scotland be cured?

▶ Look up each reference. Copy out the line/s which contain the image of disease.
▶ Make sure you understand what each one means, by talking about them. Again write notes on your discussion.
▶ You can use your notes as the basis of an essay on imagery in *Macbeth*.

BEHIND THE WORDS

EXPLAINING POEMS

This unit gives you the opportunity to read, talk, and write about poems.

It is not an easy job to say what you think a poem means, and to learn to describe the special way in which poets use language.

The section is organised so that you can work with other people in your class to share the different ideas you have before attempting to do the writing which explains the poetry you study.

Blind spots

Work in a group.

Read the poem by D. H. Lawrence.

Some words have been removed from the poem and have been listed beneath it.

The work of the group is to discuss and agree where the words fit in the spaces marked ****. Be prepared to explain your choices. This is called a cloze exercise.

Outside the house an ****(1) tree hung its terrible ****(2),
And at night when the wind rose, the ****(3) of the tree
Shrieked and ****(4) the wind, as a ship's
Weird ****(5) in a storm shrieks hideously.

Within the house two ****(6) arose, a slender lash
****(7) she-delirious rage, and the dreadful sound
Of a ****(8) thong booming and bruising, until it had drowned
The other voice in a ****(9) of blood, 'neath the ****(10) of the ash.

D. H. Lawrence

These are the words to discuss.

rigging	silence	whips	male	noise
ash	whistling	slashed	lash	voices

Next, your group should discuss the list of titles for this poem on the following page.

All of them are possible titles, but, like the poet, you will have to decide on one of them.

Keep notes to show why the one you choose is the best in the opinion of the group.

Voices in the Wind *The Tree*
The Ship of Night *The Marriage*
Discord in Childhood *Sound and Silence*

 Finally, use your notes to write a paragraph which explains why the title chosen by your group is suitable.

A further idea

 Choose a short poem from an anthology and write a cloze version of it.

Also prepare three or four alternative titles as well as the original.

Try it out on a group of friends and write a brief report of how they managed the exercise.

Behind the words

Reservation

Acres of white stars
       white eyes
          glare
as cold
and cruel as the stare

of the trooper
    in blue
       who said
       'You
       will live there'.

Our map was made
of skies and suns, of rain and wind and hills.

But they shape the land with
                lies
                guns
                and dry dollar bills.

Think of us.
We and the stars
            are still.

We see
their wagons pass,
their hard wheels
crush the grass,
the plains grass,
            straight and tall.

Our world grows small.

David Marigold

The poet says . . .

I wrote 'Reservation' when I learnt some of the details about how the United States Government used the cavalry troopers to destroy the Indian nations in the last century.

I was shocked by the cruelty of the massacres, and I realised that reservations were nothing more than prison camps. The tribes were forced to stay in these camps completely cut off from their natural way of life. Many were starved to death, executed, or deliberately infected with diseases — like smallpox.

This poem represents the thoughts of one Indian woman sitting alone. She watches the wagons pass by the camp, heading for the open country where she and her people can't go. She looks up and sees the stars in the freedom of the sky, and they remind her of the eyes of the U.S. soldier who told her family where they would have to live. She thinks bitterly of how the strangers are changing the face of the beloved land.

I chose words like 'acres', 'map', and 'world' because the tribes were deprived of vast areas of land. I hoped that the idea of the wagon wheels crushing the grass would help the readers imagine the army crushing the natural way of life of the Indian peoples.

I tried to arrange the lines so that they looked interesting. Sometimes I've broken them up because it felt right, because it seemed to fit in with the emotions of the woman's thoughts. Sometimes I've put words by themselves on a line to give them more emphasis. Not every line rhymes because I wanted the rhymes to feel natural rather than forced, so I made up my own rules as I went along. The poem went through lots of changes until I was satisfied — I suppose there were ten or eleven versions of it.

Here is one of the earlier versions.

Acres
(Miles) of white stars
   White eyes shine stare
as cold
and cruel as the (grin) glare
of the trooper blue trooper in blue
     who said
     you will live there
Our map was made
of sun and rain, of sky and wind
Skies and sun, wind and rain

and we feel the beat
of beasts feet in the silence
of the days heat.

Their map is made of
   lies, guns, and dry
   dollar bills.

Think of us.
We see their wagons pass
Whose iron hard wheels.

  Crush the grass
straight and tall
  the plains grass.

Our large world
Our world grows small.

(margin notes)
Stone eyes /
with stones

Shaping the land

iron tracks — horizons.

132

Dreams

I stand in a parking lot
the sun shines,
    my throat is parched
A red van with a pink rose
painted on the side
    drives slowly up to me,
        I step in
A fair-haired man with a stubbly beard
    hands me a cup from a flask
    cracks into it an egg
    and with a wrinkled hand
    draws up the transparent white
it is drugged I know
    Don't! my conscience cries
    But I drink
A fiendish grin spreads across his evil face
'You fool' he cries
'You fool'
    His evil green eyes glint in the sun
    My head spins as I listen to the echo
'You fooooooool!'
    His eyes fall out and crack like glass on the floor
    All that is left where his eyes were is EMPTINESS
The shining pieces of green eye
grow together to form a tortoise,
    no, a turtle,
growing larger and larger
    it opens its gigantic jaws
    out of the door I dash
    I run and run
I'm being chased
I don't dare look back . . .
    I WAKE

Miriam Bindman

The poet says . . .

My poem is based on a real dream. I had been thinking about it for many days, and when one day in English my teacher told us to write a poem about a dream, I could immediately start to write.

Writing the poem was like describing the picture I had in my mind of the dream.

I can remember in my primary school when I was about seven, a teacher once made a film of everyday school life. One part that I was in showed me putting down my shirt while changing for P.E. When the film was finished the teacher showed it backwards, so it looked as if my hand was a vacuum cleaner and the shirt came up to my hand. This is what gave me the idea of the man drawing up the egg whites in the poem. The poem is more or less an accurate account of the dream, except for the egg white idea and the real dream was much longer.

Both poets have written short explanations to help readers to understand the experiences and ideas which lie behind the words of their poems.

The explanations include:
▶ identifying unexpected memories and how a use was found for them
▶ the choice of special vocabulary and phrases
▶ the way the poem has been arranged.

Thinking about poems

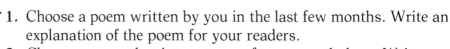

1. Choose a poem written by you in the last few months. Write an explanation of the poem for your readers.
2. Choose a poem that interests you from an anthology. Write an introduction which would help another reader to enjoy the poem.
3. Write a brief account of an important moment in your life. Use this as the basis for writing a poem about it.
4. Why are some poems hard to understand? Choose a poem which is really difficult. Make a list of all those things which are problems. Perhaps the ideas are unclear or the imagery is hard to unravel. Or perhaps the vocabulary is strange to you or the subject-matter seems to be completely outside your experience. Finally, use this list to write a few paragraphs explaining what the difficulties are. Continue for one or two more paragraphs in which you attempt to guess or explain what you think the poem is about. Don't worry about admitting you're confused by it. So are many adults expert at reading poems!

What's the difference?

A chart has been made of 'Autumn Song' by Ted Hughes (below). On the left hand side each stanza has been reduced to a simple prose explanation or 'headline'.

In pairs or in a group, discuss each stanza in order.

▶ What has the poet done that is different from the short prose explanation?

Make notes as you go through.

Use your notes to write one or two paragraphs. Explain the special ideas and techniques used to make the ordinary event of the arrival of Autumn into something much more dramatic.

Autumn: prose	Autumn Song: poem
On a certain day	There came a day that caught the summer Wrung its neck Plucked it And ate it.
The leaves begin to fall from the trees	Now what shall I do with the trees? The day said, the day said. Strip them bare, strip them bare. Let's see what is really there.
The sun begins to give less heat	And what shall I do with the sun? The day said, the day said. Roll him away till he's cold and small. He'll come back rested if he comes back at all.

Birds begin to migrate. Those that stay need food.	And what shall I do with the birds? The day said, the day said. The birds I've frightened, let them flit, I'll hang out pork for the brave tomtit.
Seeds fall to the ground.	And what shall I do with the seed? The day said, the day said. Bury it deep, see what it's worth. See if it can stand the earth.
People enjoy the fruits of the harvest.	What shall I do with the people? The day said, the day said. Stuff them with apple and black-berry pie — They'll love me then till the day they die.
This was the first day of Autumn.	There came this day and he was autumn. His mouth was wide And red as a sunset. His tail was an icicle.

Read 'November Story' by Vernon Scannell.

Make a poem/prose chart for each stanza.

Your prose explanation should be kept very simple — not much longer than a 'headline' — but should be as accurate as possible about the meaning of the stanzas.

Write a paragraph explaining the techniques used by Scannell to dramatise a very ordinary event.

Have the Hughes and Scannell poems got any techniques in common? What are they?

You now have enough material to write an essay about the poems. Your essay should include:
▶ what each poem is about
▶ how the poets have used imagery
▶ in what way the poems are similar
▶ which poem you prefer, or reasons why you are not keen on either of them.

November Story

The evening had caught cold;
   Its eyes were blurred.
It had a dripping nose
   And its tongue was furred.

I sat in a warm bar
   After the day's work;
November snuffled outside,
   Greasing the sidewalk.

But soon I had to go
   Out into the night
Where shadows prowled the alleys,
   Hiding from the light.

But light shone at the corner
  On the pavement where
A man had fallen over
  Or been knocked down there.

His legs on the slimed concrete
  Were splayed out wide;
He had been propped against a lamp-post;
  His head lolled to one side.

A victim of crime or accident,
  An image of fear,
He remained quite motionless
  As I drew near.

Then a thin voice startled silence
  From a doorway close by
Where an urchin hid from the wind:
  'Spare a penny for the guy!'

I gave the boy some money
  And hastened on.
A voice called, 'Thank you guv'nor!'
  And the words upon

The wincing air seemed strange —
  So hoarse and deep —
As if the guy had spoken
  In his restless sleep.

Vernon Scannell

Breakline ———————————————————————

The next poem was written during the International Year of the Disabled. A deaf and blind man and his helper visited Jim Mulligan's school to meet children.

Here is an earlier version of the poem.

Yesterday I witnessed a miracle:
A man with his ear in the palm of his hand,
A woman with her tongue
On the tip of her finger.

She touch-typed on skin.
Her silent words and pictures slid
Up fibres to his brain.
Then this man heard.
Then this man, his eyes cameras without film, saw,
And his voice shouted his reply.

And here is Jim Mulligan's final version.

Yesterday I witnessed a miracle:
A man with his ear in the palm of his hand,
A woman with her tongue on the tip
Of her finger.
She touch-typed on skin.
Her silent words and pictures slid
Up fibres to his brain.
Then this man —
Heard.
This man —
His eyes, cameras without film —
Saw,
And his voice shouted
His reply.

ʾke many writers, Jim Mulligan finds it difficult to leave his poems alone, even several years after they have been published. This is what he says about this one:

I'm still satisfied with the imagery I've used to explain the miracle of communication that took place. And the tone still seems to be right. Writing a non-rhymed poem gives you the freedom to play around with the 'feel' of a poem. I'm always amazed at the difference it can make for the reader simply by laying the words out in a slightly different pattern.

What is this 'difference'?

 Work in pairs.

Discuss the two versions to decide whether altering the line arrangement has made the poem
▶ easier to read

▶ easier to understand
▶ 'feel' different? What in particular?

Keep some very brief notes of your discussion.

Experimenting with line-breaks

(a) Select *one* of the following:
▶ a story written by you
▶ a printed and published novel or short story
▶ a non-fiction information book (e.g. on a hobby or topic)
▶ a school textbook on either history, biology, geography, social studies, or home economics.

Select the opening five lines of a chapter anywhere in the book. It doesn't matter if it's dull. If it's your own story it will be the first five lines.

Then, experiment with breaking the prose lines up so that they *look* like a poem on the page. You might wish to do two or three versions to see which one is the most effective.

What difference does it make for the reader? Again, write some very brief notes explaining how things have changed.

(b) *Either* choose a poem which you have written previously *or* write a new one on any subject you wish. Do at least two versions with different line-breaks. Write a few lines explaining which version of your poem you prefer, and why.

Your conclusions

You now have enough material to present a unit about the way poems are presented visually.

Using the notes you have made, your essay could include:
▶ the two versions of Jim Mulligan's poem and your comments on the differences
▶ a copy of the five lines of prose and your experiments and comments
▶ the versions of your own poem and the explanation of your own preference.

If you wish to extend your essay, select a non-rhymed poem from an anthology. Write a paragraph which comments on the effectiveness of the line arrangement.

Out of step

The poem by Brian Lee has been printed below so that the stanzas are not in their correct sequence.

Your task is to discuss and agree to an order which makes sense. It is possible that you will discover more than one version, and your group will have to decide which it prefers.

This way of working will help you to discuss the poem in detail.

The stanzas are numbered for you to record your sequence.

1.   And kneel there for ages shivering with cold
      My bare feet on the bare lino,
    An ear to the keyhole, holding my breath —
      What is it that makes me so bold?

2.   Though it's against all the rules, I still dare
      To shuffle right up to the door,
    Drawn on by murmurs I can't understand,
      The rumour of Truth in the air,

3.   Sometimes at night I crawl out of my bed,
      And tiptoe on to the landing,
    Because I'm *sure* they've been talking about me,
      And how I want to know what they've said!

4.   And I'll only find out by playing this game,
      What they think of me, what I am;
    Not knowing's much more than I can put up with,
      And asking them — just isn't the same.

5.   Doing wrong — and the dark — the sensation
      Of finding it all out at last;
    The things they don't say, the things they won't tell —
      It's all a shocking temptation:

6.   I crane and I stretch, then, if I can't hear
      I creep softly down to the hall,
    — But mind the creaks on steps three and eleven! —
      Heart thumping, mouth dry, with something like fear.

When you have finished, discuss what might be a good title for the poem. You will probably decide on three or four possibilities. Make a note of them.

This task will help you to consider what the poem is about.

Discuss these further aspects of the poem.
▶ What would you say is the age and sex of the speaker in the poem? What information helped you to decide?
▶ Who could be talking behind the door?
▶ Do you feel this is a realistic situation? Does it connect up with experiences in your life which are similar if not identical?
▶ In your opinion, is this poem written for adults or children? How did you reach this decision?

Reporting back

 Prepare a spoken report to make to the rest of your class.
It should include:
▶ reading the poem in the sequence decided by the group
▶ an explanation of why one or two of your titles are appropriate
▶ the opinions discussed in answer to No. 3 above
▶ the group's like or dislike of the poem, and the reasons for this.

You must organise who is going to make the report. Will it be one person on behalf of the whole group? Or will you share out bits between each other?

This unit concentrates on talking and writing that seeks to persuade.

It centres on a campaign either for or against experiments on animals. While care has been taken to provide a balance of source material, the task of persuading someone to adopt or change their opinions may well require you to take one side or another.

The activities in this unit could equally well be used on other controversial issues either national or international — such as the nuclear issue, or a local issue such as the siting of a new bypass or motorway. If you want to choose one of these, you will need to collect your own material.

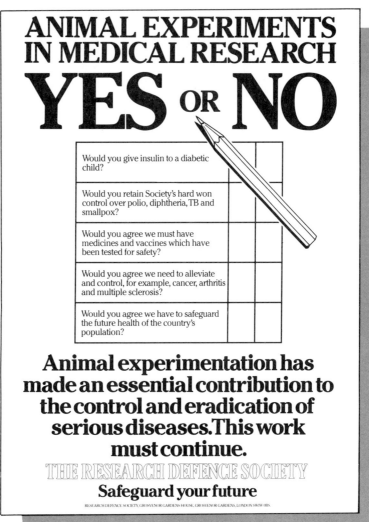

The Cancer Research Scandal

Beagle dog with implanted cancerous tumours. Photo taken in New York laboratory, but similar research is going on in Britain. © Jon Evans, F.R.G.S.

Every year in Britain over 140,000 people die from cancer. Many of these cancers are due to environmental factors and are therefore preventable.

Cancer-causing agents are in the food we eat, the drugs we take, the cigarettes we smoke and the air we breathe. Vast sums of money have been spent by the cancer charities in doing research which involves artificially inducing tumours in animals and then seeking cures for these cancers. Little money has been used to study the causes of cancer in man.

In Britain the cancer charities have between them assets of £44 million and a yearly expenditure of over £15 million. According to scientific literature, a very high percentage of cancers are preventable, and yet less than 2% of the funds of cancer charities are spent on cancer education for prevention.

What I think about animal experiments

Look at the following twelve statements and decide whether there are any that you definitely do not agree with.

(a) It is wrong to test cosmetics on animals.
(b) The only way of finding out if a new shampoo or other cosmetic is safe is to test it on animals first.
(c) We have more than enough cosmetic products already. There is no need to develop any more.
(d) I wouldn't buy a product that I didn't know was safe and I can only be sure if it has been thoroughly tested first.

(e) It is better that drugs are tested on animals before using them on human beings.

(f) Many of the advances made by modern medicine, like the eradication of smallpox, depended on animal experiments.

(g) Whatever the risks any experiments should be only carried out on human beings and not on animals.

(h) Animal experiments are unfortunately essential.

(i) We should only use animals for genuine medical experiments, such as finding a cure for cancer.

(j) Doctors are confused by the number of similar drugs available.

(k) There should be no experiments on animals for any reason.

(l) It cannot be right to make animals suffer for our convenience.

What you and a friend think

Now you need to work with another person. Consider the questions again and try to place them in three categories:

1. We agree with this statement
2. We disagree with this statement
3. We are not sure what we feel about this statement.

It is best if you can agree with each other and to make a common list. However if this proves to be impossible you may have to make individual lists.

What the class thinks

Now, using your replies to those statements, a list of your class's attitudes on animal experiments can be put together.

Using a block graph would be a good way of displaying these attitudes.

It will be interesting to see if there are any shifts of opinion while working on this unit.

The arguments for and against — in more detail

There are many shades of opinion for and against using animals in experiments. The extracts which follow will give you an idea of the spread of opinion.

Do you know the facts about animal experiments?

Here are just a few of them.

1. Over 67,000 animals die every week in British laboratories and a proportion of the experiments clearly have no relevance to the treatment of human disease and cannot be said to be essential for the saving or prolonging of life or the alleviation of suffering.
2. Animals are used for testing of oven-cleaners, lipsticks, weedkillers, crayons, candles, drugs, shampoos, floor polish, weapons, paint, golf balls, anti-freeze; the list is endless. Animals are also being increasingly used in psychological and behavioural experiments.
3. Home Office figures state that 3,497,335 experiments were performed on live animals during 1984, 79 per cent conducted without an anaesthetic at any stage; 1,843,915 experiments were performed by commercial concerns.
4. There are 21,000 persons licensed under the Cruelty to Animals Act 1876 to perform experiments on living animals and 499 premises registered for experiments.
5. The National Anti-Vivisection Society realises regretfully that vivisection will not be abolished overnight, and our policy is a practical 'step by step' one aimed at phasing out all animal experiments as quickly as possible.
6. People steal cats and dogs for sale to vivisection laboratories. Never let your pet out alone — it may be stolen for research.
7. Shampoos are instilled into the eyes of rabbits, leading to severe swelling, discharge, and often the total destruction of the cornea. During 1984 17,512 living animals were used to test cosmetics and toiletries.
8. Some manufacturers of cosmetics do *not* test their products on living animals and these cosmetics have been in use for many years; which proves that safe cosmetics can be manufactured for the general public without experiments on living animals.
9. During 1984 2,166 animals were used to test tobacco and its substitutes.
10. No independent observer has the right of entry to a laboratory to witness an experiment on a living animal — not even an RSPCA Inspector or a Member of Parliament. If these tests will not give rise to public concern, why is this shroud of secrecy necessary?
11. The last full-scale Government Inquiry into the whole practice of animal experimentation reported in 1912.
12. In some areas of research there are alternatives to experiments on living animals — tissue culture, cell culture, organ culture, computers, mathematical models, etc., techniques which are held to be safer, cheaper, and more reliable than using living animals.

13. The National Anti-Vivisection Society stimulates, sponsors, and supports medical and scientific research projects not involving experiments on live animals through a department of the Society, known as the Lord Dowdling Fund. The Fund has already awarded nearly £500,000 in grants.
14. Drugs such as Thalidomide, Eraldin, and Opren were passed safe for human use after extensive tests on animals.

From a National Anti-Vivisection Society leaflet

Can medicine advance without experiments on animals?

When I started training as a young doctor, I felt the ultimate goal of my endeavours would be the successful grafting of organs to young people dying of malfunction of the organs in question, restoring them to a long spell of worthwhile life. It seemed clear that to do this it would be necessary to remove organs from the dead and to be able to combat the body's tendency to reject grafts, animal experimentation would be needed. Now we seem to be approaching this object in kidney care; kidney grafts are functioning more than twenty years after transplantation, hearts and livers after 14 years and pancreases after 4 years. Unfortunately, many patients still do not do well and there are important difficulties to overcome. The two main obstacles to progress are lack of organ donation and opposition to experiments on animals.

Concerning the use of animals in experiments, how easy it is to play on the emotions — a rat receiving an injection or a dog being operated on can be, and often have been, portrayed as acts of sadistic cruelty, when in fact most scientists love animals and have pets of their own and will not experiment on animals if alternatives are available. Great care is taken to minimise pain by the use of general anaesthesia and analgesic drugs. Sensational reporting has inadvertently glorified criminal acts of violent antivivisectionists, encouraging them to perpetrate further outrages, which terrorise scientists to silence. Opposition is not voiced for fear of attacks against the individual who has dared to question the antivivisectionists.

If the public wishes to have the advantages of modern medicine, for example antibiotics and insulin, then experiments on animals have to be accepted. The only way to avoid hypocrisy if you really do not wish to exploit animals, is to eschew all modern powerful and effective medical treatment when you or your family are ill and avoid meat, fish and perhaps eggs and wear and use no leather.

When I was a student there were 20,000 tragic deaths mostly in young people, from tuberculosis and many other patients were maimed from poliomyelitis having to spend their lives ventilated in an iron lung. These diseases are no longer a scourge in the United Kingdom.

Smallpox and diphtheria used to be common causes of death in children and these have been eliminated. The ability to cure the most dangerous common infections, the successful repair of many heart defects, the rehabilitation of thousands of patients suffering from kidney disease are possible solely because of experiments on animals. Diabetes is treatable because insulin was discovered by Banting and Best in surgical experiments in dogs. The dog was also used to develop heart and transplantation surgery.

Unfortunately, there are still many diseases which cause suffering and death in the young, for example the childhood cancers and leukaemias, and if progress is to be made at a reasonable price, the public must accept experiments with animals.

Most of us love animals but eat meat and wear leather shoes. We accept medical treatment based on animal experiments and expect further advances in the future. Wild animals prey on each other, domesticated carnivorous pets — the dog and cat — need meat to maintain health. An ethical and humane analysis of our emotions concerning animals is not easy but the fact that most important medical advances have followed animal experiments cannot be denied, nor the need for further animal experiments if medical advances are to continue as most of us would wish. It is a sad comment on contemporary society that discussion and argument of these matters have been answered by abuse and terrorist bombs.

Professor Roy Calne (extracts from a lecture in November 1983)

Analysis of the articles

 Working with a partner, or in a group, pick out what you think are the three best points made by each writer. Now think of questions you would like to put to each writer which you hope either will show up weaknesses in their argument or clarify points you are not sure about.

Planning a campaign: putting over your case

The following activities assume you are running a campaign to persuade people of the rightness of *your* point of view on this subject. You will be trying to persuade people to change their minds or to make up their minds.

You should now decide for which side you wish to campaign!

Some possibilities you should consider

▶ Letters to your Member of Parliament or Local Councillor or local newspaper explaining why animal experiments should be supported, or curtailed, or banned altogether. Councillors are usually busy people, so it is important not to write a long and rambling letter.

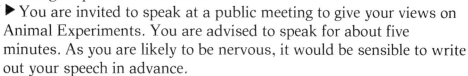

▶ Group/class discussions with one or two people putting the opposing views. You could give a presentation to your class or by arrangement to another class or to your tutor group.

▶ Design a leaflet to distribute to Saturday shoppers.

▶ Design a poster or a T shirt.

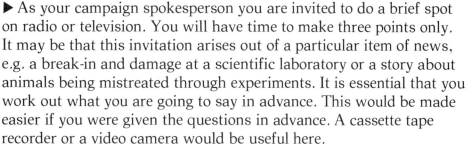

▶ You are invited to speak at a public meeting to give your views on Animal Experiments. You are advised to speak for about five minutes. As you are likely to be nervous, it would be sensible to write out your speech in advance.

▶ As your campaign spokesperson you are invited to do a brief spot on radio or television. You will have time to make three points only. It may be that this invitation arises out of a particular item of news, e.g. a break-in and damage at a scientific laboratory or a story about animals being mistreated through experiments. It is essential that you work out what you are going to say in advance. This would be made

easier if you were given the questions in advance. A cassette tape recorder or a video camera would be useful here.

▶ An article, which puts your case, for a magazine.

Are there limits to a campaign of protest?

All the suggested activities in the previous section are perfectly legal. However some campaigns go further than this.

The activities of the Animal Liberation Front (ALF), such as breaking into scientific laboratories and releasing animals, have caught the headlines. The ALF feel that writing letters to Members of Parliament, writing books and articles, demonstrating against animal experiments (and the treatment of animals in general) has not produced sufficient change, so some campaigners have chosen more direct action.

We have no wish to hurt people and we are not against those whose shops we attacked. But we have become frustrated with the way things are. Legal marches and demonstrations have not been recognised by the Government.

Speaker for a Kent group of ALF

Scientists involved in animal experiments have had their cars and homes spray-painted.

Certainly the people who have attacked my home and those of a growing number of my colleagues have no interest in debate or they would not remain clandestine. Was the person who sent a letter bomb to Professor Roy Calne interested in debate? Or the ones who recently broke into the home of the Managing Director of the Wickham Toxicology Laboratory and floored him with an iron bar? I do not think so.

Sir John Vane, 1984

Are there limits to the types of protest that ought to be used?

What do you think they are?

Would you approve of any of the following four actions?

1. 16 January, 1983, Guildford Surrey
   Anti-vivisection raiders cut their way into the grounds of the Ministry of Agriculture's Infestation Control Laboratory in the early hours of the morning and rescued two foxes from their cages and painted anti-vivisection slogans on the buildings.
2. 12 February 1983, Nottingham
   Locks glued at two offices of Boots' animal research labs and two windows smashed using catapults. Main plate glass window and window in door, of the town centre branch of Boots, smashed by a catapult.
3. 4 March 1983
   Two lurcher dogs rescued from premises of man who was going to send them to a vivisection lab. The dogs were in poor condition and covered in sores. They are now in good homes.
4. 21 April 1983, Derby
   Machine valued at about £5,000, used for killing animals for dissection, removed from Lonsdale College and destroyed.

Where do you draw the line on campaigning?

This question would be best discussed in a small group of up to six people. Your conclusions could then be reported back to the whole class.

Have your views changed?

Do all the class still hold the same opinions about animal experimentation as they did at the start of this unit?

13

ON THE RACK

WRITING FOR A MAGAZINE

In this unit you will write a number of magazine articles.

You will need a collection of magazines to remind you what they consist of: the articles, their audiences, and their assumptions about their readers. It will also give you ideas on layout and style when you come to write. It should be possible (and cheap) to collect out-of-date copies from your local newsagent as well as any old copies you may have at home.

Types

Nowadays there are hundreds of magazine titles. Look on the shelves of your local newsagent. You will find an even wider selection in a large town or city-centre newsagent. You will find magazines on fishing, fashion, football, food, swimming, snooker, style, netball, needlework, computers, cookery, music, finance, politics, tennis . . .

Some magazines are devoted to a *single interest* like snooker, cooking or tennis. There are even magazines written for a particular model of computer, a type of fish (like trout), or a single popular music group. These types of magazines are usually very detailed and treat their readers as experts and enthusiasts.

Others are *general interest* magazines which cover a wide range of subjects, in less detail, to attract a wide readership. Most women's and current affairs magazines are like this.

Some are aimed at a *particular audience*; for instance there are style magazines for teenagers and the early twenties, magazines for young children, or publications for a particular institution like a school, a company, or a fire brigade. There are usually a variety of subjects in these magazines.

 Working in pairs or groups compile a list of twenty magazine titles, noting the type of magazine they are.

A visit to your local newsagent may help you.

Next, in pairs or groups, see if you can fit these titles into the following categories:
▶ single interest
▶ general interest/wider audience
▶ particular audience
▶ none of these.

You may find that some titles fit into more than one category; this does not matter.

▶ Draw a chart, using Table 1 as a guide.

Table 1. Types of Magazine

Single interest	General interest	Wide audience	Particular audience	None of these

Inside pages

Whatever the different readership or particular interest, magazines have many similar items.

They often have:
▶ an editorial or opinion page
▶ pages of news
▶ a letters page
▶ a problem page
▶ interviews
▶ reviews.

The subjects change, the look of magazines differs enormously, and so does their readerships, but they have basic ingredients in common.

Now look through a selection of magazines and pick out the basic ingredients.

Choose six different magazines and make a list of their contents. Draw a chart using Table 2.

Try to choose magazines with very different subjects. What articles or features do they have in common?

Table 2.   Does the magazine contain . . . ?

Type of Article

Magazine Title	Editorial/Opinion	Letters	Advice/Problem Page	News	Reviews	How to Do It (explanations)	Interviews	Adverts	List of Contents	List of Staff who produced magazine

Assumptions

Editors of magazines have to make assumptions about the make-up and interests of their readers.

Choose one magazine that is written for your age group. What assumptions have the editors made about you? Have they got it right?

In pairs or groups discuss the following questions. Make notes during your discussion; they will be used for an essay later on in this section.
▶ What subjects are covered in the magazine?
▶ What interests do they think you have?
▶ How does the magazine address you, the reader?
▶ What do the models in the adverts look like? Are they wearing clothes you would wear?

▶ What are the people shown in the magazine doing?
▶ Do you think the magazine is written mainly for boys or girls or both sexes?

Using the magazine you have been discussing, write an essay which gives information about the way it presents young people. Your essay should include comments about the content and illustrations, and your opinion as a reader.

This essay could be photocopied and sent, with a letter of explanation, to the editor of the magazine.

Planning your articles

Having looked at a number of commercial magazines, you are now going to write some articles of your own. Before you start writing you will need to make a number of decisions.

Subject and audience

▶ Will your articles be all on the same subject or theme?
▶ Will they be based on a special interest or hobby of yours?
▶ Will they be based on a particular theme — for instance, the supernatural, looking after animals, or romance?
▶ Or will you be writing a series of articles of topical interest for a class or school magazine?
▶ What sort of audience are you writing for?
▶ Are you expecting your audience to be knowledgeable or to know little about your subject?
▶ Will your articles appeal to both sexes?

Content and style

You can choose from this list of different types of article. Try at least three.
▶ *editorial/opinion*
This type of article often comes at the beginning of a magazine. Here the editor gives an opinion, on a particular subject or issue, or someone else is invited to do so. The opinion and the subject are often controversial and the article short and 'punchy'.

▶ *news* — about people, events, what's happening, up to date information etc.

▶ *interviews*: who to interview?

Anyone and everybody!

The famous, the infamous, ordinary people, the stars, your friends. You can interview anyone. Remember to think about the questions you want to ask before you begin the interview. Will you want to use a tape recorder?

▶ *reviews*

What is reviewed? New products — new events. Books   Cars Records Films Plays Clothes Shops Restaurants Sporting Events Computers Motor Bikes Concerts Fashion Shows almost anything you can think of.

▶ *letters*

The letters page is often the most popular page in a magazine. It allows readers the space in which to complain, give praise, express their opinions and helps them to feel that it's their magazine.

▶ *features*

These are usually articles of considerable length, in which subjects are analysed and written about in depth. Often these articles form the centrepiece of a magazine, and their titles are highlighted on the magazine cover. You may wish to write an article based on your findings and discussion on assumptions in the previous section.

▶ *how to do it*

Many magazines carry full length 'How to do it' articles. These give detailed explanations on how to cook special dishes, train to run a marathon, knit a cardigan, and so on.

▶ *problem page*

Readers write in seeking advice. In some magazines readers want advice on emotional problems. Other letters, particularly in those titles devoted to a single subject, ask for advice on this particular interest. So snooker magazines give advice on tactics or what type of cue to buy. Fishing titles give help on choosing the best tackle or bait.

Will you include graphics (illustrations)?

Late extra

Once you have completed your articles, you might decide to collect together copies (keeping the originals in your course work folder) of the class's articles and turn them into a magazine of your class's writing. You could decide to select the best article from each person.

14

THE PLAY IN THE BOOK

SCRIPT-WRITING

There are a lot of differences between a written story and a play. One of the biggest differences is that the writer of a story can tell the reader what a character is thinking and feeling, but the writer of a play has to convey the same things *only* in what the actors say and do. Playwrights can't jump up on the stage and say, 'This character is nervous at the moment!' or 'This character doesn't like that character, but is trying not to show it!' The playwright has to get these messages across using only speech and actions. In this unit you can see how one writer adapted a written story for a play on television, and you can try your hand at doing the same kind of thing. The story is *Buddy*, by Nigel Hinton, and the adaptation was for a five-part serial on BBC School Television in 1986.

This is part of Chapter 13 of *Buddy*, where Buddy and his father visit Buddy's school for a parents' evening. Buddy's father is not used to this kind of occasion, because previously Buddy's mother would have gone to the school, but she has left him, and Buddy and his father are trying to get along as best they can without her. Part of the problem is that Buddy's father is dressed in full Teddy Boy dress, which is the smartest clothing he has.

1 They arrived at the school just after ten past seven. There were pupils and parents all over the school and Buddy led the way to his classroom feeling as if everyone was looking at him. He tried to stay a couple of steps ahead of his dad — not too far to let his dad know it, but enough so that people couldn't be sure they were together.

There were some chairs outside the classroom and his dad sat down while Buddy peeped through the window into the room. Colin Franks was sitting with his well-dressed parents talking to Mr Normington who was wearing a dark suit with a small red rose-bud in the buttonhole.

'It's not bad 'ere, is it?' his dad said and Buddy noticed that he was playing with the plastic bag and looking up and down the corridor, almost as if he were nervous. Buddy watched out of the corner of his eye as his dad brushed the collar of his jacket and touched the edges of his hair to make sure that it was still tidy. He wiped his hands on his trousers and then checked his nails.

'What's this Mr Normington like, then? All right, is he?'

2 That did it. His dad was scared. Mr Normington would have to lump it. He loved his dad and he didn't care who knew it. He sat down beside him and began telling him about the new block they were in — when it was built, the number of rooms, how they'd found cracks in the ceiling already — anything to stop his dad being scared.

The door opened and the Franks came out and walked off down the corridor without even glancing in the direction of Buddy and his dad.

'Next please,' Mr Normington called.

Buddy took a deep breath and led the way in.

Mr Normington was standing behind the desk. Buddy saw the eyebrows flicker and the smile freeze as he caught sight of his dad's clothes. There was a brief silence then Mr Normington pulled himself together.

'Ah, Mr Clark. How do you do?' He held his hand out and Buddy's dad went to shake it with the hand holding the plastic bag. He laughed nervously, put the bag down on Mr Normington's desk then shook hands.

'Pleased to meet you.'

'Yes, well . . . Do sit down, Mr Clark, and you, Buddy. Right, where shall we begin? The reports first, perhaps. Oh.' Mr Normington found that all his papers were under the plastic bag. Buddy leaped up and pulled the bag away and Mr Normington began reading the comments that each of the

3 teachers had made. Buddy was so tense that he barely listened, though he was dimly aware that they all sounded quite good. After every subject report Mr Normington stopped and looked at Buddy's dad who kept saying, 'Oh — nice.'

'Well,' Mr Normington said, pushing aside the reports, 'as you can see from those comments, Buddy is doing very well in 3E. We're very pleased with him.'

'Oh — nice.'

'Of course, it's a long way off yet, but we're hoping for great things from him in GCEs.'

'Oh — nice.'

'Have you talked about careers yet?'

Buddy's dad glanced at him with a slightly worried look, so Buddy butted in, 'Well, we've talked about some things but I haven't made up my mind yet.'

4 'Of course. I'm sorry, Mr Clark,' Mr Normington said, looking down at Buddy's record card, 'I can't recall what you do for a living.'

Buddy's heart raced.

'Ah, yes — here it is. Oh, you worked at Bradley's. That's closed down, hasn't it?'

'Yeah, beginning of the year. I do a bit with antiques on the side now. I'm 'oping to start a shop like what I used to 'ave.'

Buddy winced at the dropped 'h's but Mr Normington nodded and smiled.

'Well, then,' he said, 'I don't think there's much else from our end.

Unless, of course, you've got any problems at your end?'

'No, everyfink's fine,' his dad said quickly.

'Good. Good. Well, let's hope young Buddy keeps up the good work. Make sure you always supervise his prep, etcetera.'

'Prep?' his dad said, and darted a look at Buddy.

'Yes, private studies — in the evenings,' Mr Normington said.

'Oh, 'omework. Oh yes, he's good like that — always does it.'

'Not too much time wasted in front of the television?'

'We 'aven't got a telly. We . . . er . . . got rid of it.'

'Did you?' Mr Normington said, and Buddy could see he was impressed. 'Good. There's some splendid stuff on it, of course — but it can be a dreadful time-waster. Well, well — thank you for coming, Mr Clark.'

They all stood up and Buddy's dad shook hands with Mr Normington.

5 ⌈ 'By the way, how's Mrs Clark? Well, I trust.'
  | 'Oh, yeah — she's ok.'
  | 'Good. give her my regards.'
  ⌊ 'Yeah, I will.'

6 ⌈ As they walked to the door, Buddy could almost feel the relief pouring off
  ⌊ his dad.

Turning a story into a play

 If you were adapting this as a play, how would you deal with these problems? (The numbers refer to the numbered sections of the story.)

1. What stage directions would indicate that Buddy was embarrassed?
2. In the rest of this scene, how would you show that Buddy loved his father for being brave enough to come to the school?
3. Buddy doesn't say much here, so how will the audience know he is tense?
4. Buddy's father is actually unemployed. How will he speak these lines?
5. Mrs Clark has actually left home. How will he speak these lines?
6. How would you show that Buddy's Dad was relieved? Would you invent some extra dialogue to show it?

These are Nigel Hinton's own comments on adapting his story:

While I was writing *Buddy* I always saw the scenes in my head like a film so I didn't find it very difficult to adapt the book into a TV script. There were, however, two problems.

The first was time. I couldn't fit all the material from the book into a film of five short episodes. The heart of the story is really about how Buddy gets along with other people, especially his dad, so I decided to leave out things that didn't deal with that. The most obvious section to cut was the one where Buddy runs away to the country, then I looked through the book and left out smaller scenes, such as the one at the Satellite Club, that didn't directly affect the main story.

The other problem was more difficult. Quite a lot of the book deals with Buddy's thoughts and feelings rather than what he actually does or says. In a book it's easy enough to write something like 'Buddy felt lonely' or 'Buddy began to worry where his dad was' but how do you show that on film?

In the book Buddy spends a lot of time thinking about his mum and dad and wishing they were together. An actor can show that he's thinking, but he can't show what he's thinking about. So I solved the problem by writing a couple of scenes where Buddy takes out a photograph of his mum and dad and looks at it. When I wanted to show that Buddy was scared that his dad had had an accident, I wrote a scene where he goes into his dad's empty bedroom. He then goes into the bathroom and is just about to clean his teeth when he hears the distant siren of an ambulance. It only needed the actor to look up with a worried expression for the viewer to know what he's thinking about.

On another occasion I wanted to show how lonely Buddy felt and I also needed to get across the information that it was his birthday. I finally hit on the idea of getting him to ring up the Speaking Clock to suggest how desperate he was to hear someone talk, and then getting him to tell the recorded voice that it was his birthday.

That scene, like quite a number of others, is not in the book because there the same information could be given in another way. The film and the book *Buddy* tell the same story but how to tell it in pictures rather than in words often requires the writer to make changes.

Try your own adaptation

Before you read Nigel's own adaptation, try it yourself. Remember:
▶ You can cut or add dialogue.
▶ The actors will need stage directions about what to do, where to move, and how to deliver their lines.
▶ Although the scene takes about four minutes to read, your scene will have to be over in three minutes.
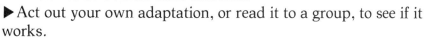▶ Act out your own adaptation, or read it to a group, to see if it works.

Part of Nigel's own adaptation follows on the next page.

SCENE FOURTEEN: *Interior: Outside 3E's classroom: Night*
  BUDDY *is sitting on a chair a couple of places away from his Dad, who is sitting on another one of the chairs arranged in the corridor. Some parents with a young girl walk along the corridor.*
  BUDDY *gets up at once to distance himself. He goes to the classroom door. The parents give* TERRY *a funny look.* TERRY *smiles ingratiatingly then starts looking at his nails. He finds some dirt and cleans it.* BUDDY *looks through the glass in the door.* MR NORMINGTON *is interviewing* EMMA GROVES *and her parents.* BUDDY *closes his eyes in despair.*

TERRY: Not bad 'ere, is it?

He plays nervously with his bag.

TERRY: What's this Mr Normington like then? All right, is he?

  BUDDY *shrugs but, sensing his Dad's discomfort, goes and sits down again — still a couple of chairs away, though.*

TERRY: Phew, blimey. (*He's really nervous.*) Never 'ad to do this before. (*He appeals to Buddy.*) I know I don't talk posh.

  BUDDY *is touched. He moves next to* TERRY.

BUDDY: Doesn't matter.
TERRY: Well.
BUDDY: You're my dad, aren't you? That's all that matters.

  TERRY *flashes a grin of thanks. The Groves family comes out and goes off without seeing* BUDDY *and* TERRY.

MR NORMINGTON: Next please.
TERRY: 'Ere goes.

  He wipes his hands nervously on his jacket and they go in. MR NORMINGTON *stands up. His smile freezes then unfreezes with difficulty.*

MR NORMINGTON: Ah, Mr Clark. How do you do?

  TERRY *holds out his plastic bag. Laughs, then dumps it on the desk and grabs* MR NORMINGTON's *hand — evidently too firmly.*

TERRY: Pleased to meet you, I'm sure.
MR NORMINGTON: Yes, well . . . Do sit down Mr Clark; and you, Buddy. Right, where shall we begin? The reports first, perhaps.

The plastic bag is on them. BUDDY *quickly grabs it.*

MR NORMINGTON: Well, this shouldn't take long — they're all very good, I'm pleased to say.
TERRY: Oh — nice.
MR NORMINGTON: Maths — 'Excellent work'. English — 'Very good work. Shows imaginative flair'.

TERRY: Oh — nice.

MR NORMINGTON *rattles through the rest.*

MR NORMINGTON: History — 'Consistently good essays'. Geography — 'Fair'. Physics — 'Works well'. Biology — 'Good work'. Sociology — 'Good'. Computer Studies — 'Good grasp of basics'. Art — 'Not particularly talented but tries hard'. French — 'Good accent. Good grasp of grammar.' Well, not much to complain about there, is there? So, as you can see from these comments, Mr Clark, Buddy is doing very well in 3E. We're very pleased with him.

TERRY: Right brain-box, in't 'e?

EITHER

▶ Carry on where Nigel Hinton's adaptation stops. Take your play-script through to where the extract from the book ends.

OR

▶ Write your own script, in play-form, of Buddy and his father on the way home after leaving the school.

Further work

1. Try the same thing with a story, or part of a story, you've written yourself.

2. Try one of these three short scenes in book-form, or play-form, or both.

    A scene with two people, where one is in love with the other, but can't say it openly.

    A scene with two people, where one has some bad news to tell the other, but doesn't know how to break the news.

    A scene with two people, where one is being threatening and frightening to the other without ever saying anything openly.

3. Take a short scene from a book you're reading at school or at home, or from a magazine. (The book doesn't have to be fiction; it could be a true story.) Adapt it in play-form, so that the scene gets across as much as possible of what was in the original story.

4. Write a scene based on an incident in your own life — something you've seen, or that's happened to you.

15

CLOSE ENCOUNTERS

THINKING ABOUT POETRY

Comparing poems

It is often easier to talk and write about poetry by comparing two poems than by reading only one. A useful way to start writing a comparison is simply to decide which one you prefer, and perhaps to think of what you would say if you were trying to persuade someone to your point of view.

Here are five pairs of poems for you to compare. It would be best to work with a friend to talk through your thoughts about them before writing your comparisons.

Remembering

Piano

Softly, in the dusk, a woman is singing to me;
Taking me back down the vista of years, till I see
A child sitting under the piano, in the boom of the tingling strings
And pressing the small, poised feet of a mother who smiles as she sings.

In spite of myself, the insidious mastery of song
Betrays me back, till the heart of me weeps to belong
To the old Sunday evenings at home, with winter outside
And hymns in the cozy parlour, the tinkling piano our guide.

So now it is vain for the singer to burst into clamour
With the great black piano appassionato. The glamour
Of childish days is upon me, my manhood is cast
Down in the flood of remembrance, I weep like a child for the past.

D. H. Lawrence

In memory of my Grandfather

Swearing about the weather he walked in
like an old tree and sat down;
his beard charred with tobacco, his voice
rough as the bark of his cracked hands.

Whenever he came it was the wrong time.
Roots spread over the hearth, tripped
whoever tried to move about the room;
the house was cramped with only furniture.

But I was glad of his coming. Only
through him could I breathe in the sun
and smell of fields. His clothes reeked
of the soil and the world outside;

geese and cows were the colour he made them,
he knew the language of birds and brought them
singing out of his beard, alive
to my blankets. He was winter and harvest.

Plums shone in his eyes when he rambled
of orchards. With giant thumbs he'd split
an apple through the core, and juice
flowed from his ripe, uncultured mouth.

Then, hearing the room clock chime,
he walked from my ceiling of farmyards
and returned to his forest of thunder;
the house regained silence and corners.

Slumped there in my summerless season
I longed for his rough hands and words
to break the restrictions of my bed,
to burst like a tree from my four walls.

But there was no chance again of miming
his habits or language. Only now,
years later in a cramped city, can I
be grateful for his influence and love.

Edward Storey

163

Fighting for your country

For the fallen
September 1914

With proud thanksgiving, a mother for her children,
England mourns for her dead across the sea.
Flesh of her flesh they were, spirit of her spirit,
Fallen in the cause of the free.

Solemn the drums thrill: Death august and royal
Sings sorrow up into immortal spheres.
There is music in the midst of desolation
And a glory that shines upon our tears.

They went with songs to the battle, they were young,
Straight of limb, true of eye, steady and aglow.
They were staunch to the end against odds uncounted,
They fell with their faces to the foe.

They shall not grow old, as we that are left grow old:
Age shall not weary them, nor the years condemn.
At the going down of the sun and in the morning
We will remember them.

They mingle not with their laughing comrades again;
They sit no more at familiar tables of home;
They have no lot in our labour of the day-time;
They sleep beyond England's foam.

But where our desires are and our hopes profound,
Felt as a well-spring that is hidden from sight,
To the innermost heart of their own land they are known
As the stars are known to the Night;

As the stars that shall be bright when we are dust,
Moving in marches upon the heavenly plain,
As the stars that are starry in the time of our darkness,
To the end, to the end, they remain.

Laurence Binyon

Dulce et decorum est

Bent double, like old beggars under sacks,
Knock-kneed, coughing like hags, we cursed through sludge,
Till on the haunting flares we turned our backs,
And towards our distant rest began to trudge.
Men marched asleep. Many had lost their boots,
But limped on, blood-shod. All went lame, all blind;
Drunk with fatigue; deaf even to the hoots
Of gas-shells dropping softly behind.

Gas! Gas! Quick, boys! — An ecstasy of fumbling,
Fitting the clumsy helmets just in time,
But someone still was yelling out and stumbling
And flound'ring like a man in fire or lime.
Dim through the misty panes and thick green light,
As under a green sea, I saw him drowning.

In all my dreams before my helpless sight
He plunges at me, guttering, choking, drowning.

If in some smothering dreams, you too could pace
Behind the wagon that we flung him in,
And watch the white eyes writhing in his face,
His hanging face, like a devil's sick of sin,
If you could hear, at every jolt, the blood
Come gargling from the froth-corrupted lungs
Bitter as the cud
Of vile, incurable sores on innocent tongues, —
My friend, you would not tell with such high zest
To children ardent for some desperate glory,
The old lie: *Dulce et decorum est*
Pro patria mori.

Wilfred Owen

The power of time

Uncle Time

Uncle Time is a ole, ole man . . .
All year long 'im wash 'im foot in de sea
long, lazy years on de wet san'
and shake de coconut tree dem
quiet-like wid 'im sea-win' laughter,
scraping away de lan' . . .

Uncle Time is a spider-man, cunnin' and cool,
him tell you: watch de hill an yu si me.
Huhh! Fe yu yi no quick enough fe si
how 'im move like mongoose; man, yu tink 'im fool?

Me Uncle Time smile black as sorrow;
'im voice is sof' as bamboo leaf
but Lawd, me Uncle cruel.
When 'im play in de street
wid yu woman — watch 'im! By tomorrow
she dry as cane-fire, bitter as cassava;
an when 'im teach yu son, long after
yu walk wid stranger, an yu bread is grief.
Watch how 'im spin web roun' yu house, an creep
inside; an when 'im touch yu, weep . . .

Dennis Scott

The author's epitaph, made by himself

Even such is Time, which takes in trust
Our youth, our joys, and all we have,
And pays us but with age and dust;
Who in the dark and silent grave,
When we have wandered all our ways,
Shuts up the story of our days:
And from which earth, and grave, and dust,
The Lord shall raise me up, I trust.

Walter Ralegh

Exaggerating

My mistress' eyes are nothing like the sun,
Coral is far more red than her lips red,
If snow be white, why then her breasts are dun,
If hairs be wires, black wires grow on her head.
I have seen roses damasked, red and white,
But no such roses see I in her cheeks,
And in some perfumes is there more delight
Than in the breath that from my mistress reeks.
I love to hear her speak, yet well I know
That music hath a far more pleasing sound,
I grant I never saw a goddess go,
My mistress when she walks treads on the ground.
   And yet, by heaven, I think my love as rare
   As any she belied with false compare.

William Shakespeare

O, my luve's like a red, red rose,
   That's newly sprung in June:
O, my luve's like the melodie
   That's sweetly played in tune.

As fair art thou, my bonie lass,
   So deep in luve am I:
And I will luve thee still, my dear,
   Till a' the seas gang dry.

Till a' the seas gang dry, my dear,
   And the rocks melt wi' the sun:
I will luve thee still, my dear,
   While the sands o' life shall run.

Robert Burns

London

I wander through each chartered street,
Near where the chartered Thames does flow,
And mark in every face I meet
Marks of weakness, marks of woe.

In every cry of every man,
In every infant's cry of fear,
In every voice, in every ban,
The mind-forged manacles I hear.

How the chimney-sweeper's cry
Every blackening church appals;
And the hapless soldier's sigh
Runs in blood down palace walls.

But most through midnight streets I hear
How the youthful harlot's curse
Blasts the new-born infant's tear,
And blights with plagues the marriage hearse.

William Blake

Composed upon Westminster Bridge, September 3, 1802

Earth has not anything to show more fair:
Dull would he be of soul who could pass by
A sight so touching in its majesty:
This City now doth, like a garment, wear
The beauty of the morning; silent, bare,
Ships, towers, domes, theatres, and temples lie
Open unto the fields, and to the sky;
All bright and glittering in the smokeless air.
Never did sun more beautifully steep
In his first splendour, valley, rock, or hill;
Ne'er saw I, never felt, a calm so deep!
The river glideth at his own sweet will:
Dear God! the very houses seem asleep;
And all that mighty heart is lying still!

William Wordsworth

Further work

You could use poetry anthologies to choose your own pairs of poems.

These could be:
▶ by the same author
▶ linked by theme
▶ linked by country.

If you work with a group, you could each choose a poem you like and then make comparisons, or simply write about the one you prefer.

Groups of poems

Many anthologies group poems together in sections because they have similarities in their subject-matter. For instance:

work	relationships	love
death	city life	memories
humour	observing things	animals
being alone	hopes and fears	
childhood, youth and age		

What you can do

This is a checklist of activities which you could use on groups of two or more poems:
▶ Compile your own collection of poems grouped by theme. The choice of theme is up to you.
▶ Write a poem of your own to go with the theme you've chosen.
▶ Which is your favourite poem in the group, and why?
▶ Write the best question you can to go with each poem. The question would be one you have probably asked yourself, and one whose answer you think would help another reader to understand and enjoy the poem.
▶ Most editors of anthologies write a short introduction to their book. Write an introduction for your group of poems. You could explain to the readers why the theme interests you, and explain some of the individual poems in such a way as to help the reader to appreciate why you found them interesting.

▶ Use anthologies to select four or five poems which have strong points of view or strong feelings.

 ▶ Prepare a live reading of them for your own class or for another class. You should link the readings by a few comments about the poems or why they were chosen.

▶ An alternative could be a tape-recorded poetry programme. This idea is best done with a friend or a group.

 Here is a collection of seven poems on the theme of Animals, each with a single question.

▶ You could use them for discussion work, for adding more animal poems of your own or from an anthology, or for writing about the ones you like.

The Wild Swans at Coole

The trees are in their autumn beauty,
The woodland paths are dry,
Under the October twilight the water
Mirrors a still sky;
Upon the brimming water among the stones
Are nine-and-fifty swans.

The nineteenth autumn has come upon me
Since I first made my count;
I saw, before I had well finished,
All suddenly mount
And scatter wheeling in great broken rings
Upon their clamorous wings.

I have looked upon those brilliant creatures,
And now my heart is sore.
All's changed since I, hearing at twilight,
The first time on this shore,
The bell-beat of their wings above my head,
Trod with a lighter tread.

Unwearied still, lover by lover,
They paddle in the cold
Companionable streams or climb the air;
Their hearts have not grown old;
Passion or conquest, wander where they will,
Attend upon them still.

But now they drift on the still water
Mysterious, beautiful;
Among what rushes will they build,
By what lake's edge or pool
Delight men's eyes when I awake some day
To find they have flown away?

W. B. Yeats

▶ What are the differences that the poet feels between himself and the swans?

The Darkling Thrush

I leant upon a coppice gate
    When Frost was spectre-gray,
And Winter's dregs made desolate
    The weakening eye of day.
The tangled bine-stems scored the sky
    Like strings of broken lyres,
And all mankind that haunted nigh
    Had sought their household fires.

The land's sharp features seemed to be
    The Century's corpse outleant,
His crypt the cloudy canopy,
    The wind his death-lament.
The ancient pulse of germ and birth
    Was shrunken hard and dry,
And every spirit upon earth
    Seemed fervorless as I.

At once a voice arose among
    The bleak twigs overhead
In a full-hearted evensong
    Of joy illimited;
An aged thrush, frail, gaunt, and small,
    In blast-beruffled plume,
Had chosen thus to fling his soul
    Upon the growing gloom.

So little cause for carolings
    Of such ecstatic sound
Was written on terrestrial things
    Afar or nigh around,
That I could think there trembled through
    His happy good-night air
Some blessed Hope, whereof he knew
    And I was unaware.

Thomas Hardy

▶ Half of this poem describes the landscape, not the thrush. Which do you think has the most impact on the poet?

My Cat Jeffrey

For I will consider my cat Jeffrey.
For he is the servant of the Living God, duly and daily serving
    Him.
For at the first glance of the glory of God in the east he worships in
    his way.
For this is done by wreathing his body seven times round with
    elegant quickness. . . .
For having done duty and received blessing he begins to consider
    himself.
For this he performs in ten degrees.
For first he looks upon his forepaws to see if they are clean.
For secondly he kicks up behind to clear away there.
For thirdly he works it upon stretch with the forepaws extended.
For fourthly he sharpens his paws by wood.

For fifthly he washes himself.
For sixthly he rolls upon wash.
For seventhly he fleas himself, that he may not be interrupted upon
    the beat.
For eighthly he rubs himself against a post.
    For ninthly he looks up for his instructions.
For tenthly he goes in quest of food.
For having considered God and himself he will consider his
    neighbour.
For if he meets another cat he will kiss her in kindness.
For when he takes his prey he plays with it to give it chance.

For one mouse in seven escapes by his dallying.

For when his day's work is done his business more properly begins.

For he keeps the Lord's watch in the night against the adversary.

For he counteracts the powers of darkness by his electrical skin and glaring eyes.

For he counteracts the Devil, who is death, by brisking about the life.

For in his morning orisons he loves the sun and the sun loves him.

For he is of the tribe of tiger.

For the cherub cat is a term of the angel tiger.

For he has the subtlety and hissing of a serpent, which in goodness he suppresses.

For he will not do destruction, if he is well fed, neither will he spit without provocation.

For he purrs in thankfulness, when God tells him he's a good cat.

For he is an instrument for the children to learn benevolence upon.

For every house is incomplete without him and a blessing is lacking in the spirit. . . .

Christopher Smart

▶ What makes a poet write about a domestic cat in this way?

'A bird came down the walk'

A bird came down the walk:
He did not know I saw;
He bit an angle-worm in halves
And ate the fellow, raw.

And then he drank a dew
From a convenient grass,
And then hopped sidewise to the wall
To let a beetle pass.

He glanced with rapid eyes
That hurried all around —
They looked like frightened beads, I thought.
He stirred his velvet head

Like one in danger; cautious,
I offered him a crumb,
And he unrolled his feathers
And rowed him softer home

Than oars divide the ocean,
Too silver for a seam,
Or butterflies, off banks of noon,
Leap, plashless, as they swim.

Emily Dickinson

▶What aspects of the bird have impressed the poet most?

View of a Pig

The pig lay on a barrow dead.
It weighed, they said, as much as three men.
Its eyes closed, pink white eyelashes.
Its trotters stuck straight out.

Such weight and thick pink bulk
Set in death seemed not just dead.
It was less than lifeless, further off.
It was like a sack of wheat.

I thumped it without feeling remorse.
One feels guilty insulting the dead,
Walking on graves. But this pig
Did not seem able to accuse.

It was too dead. Just so much
A poundage of lard and pork.
Its last dignity had entirely gone.
It was not a figure of fun.

Too dead now to pity.
To remember its life, din, stronghold
Of earthly pleasure as it had been,
Seemed a false effort, and off the point.

Too deadly factual. Its weight
Oppressed me — how could it be moved?
And the trouble of cutting it up!
The gash in its throat was shocking, but not pathetic.

Once I ran at a fair in the noise
To catch a greased piglet
That was faster and nimbler than a cat,
Its squeal was the rending of metal.

Pigs must have hot blood, they feel like ovens.
Their bite is worse than a horse's —
They chop a half-moon clean out.
They eat cinders, dead cats.

Distinctions and admirations such
As this one was long finished with.
I stared at it a long time. They were going to scald it,
Scald it and scour it like a doorstep.

Ted Hughes

▶ In verse six, the poet writes 'Too deadly factual'. What does he mean?

Song of the Battery Hen

We can't grumble about accommodation:
we have a new concrete floor that's
always dry, four walls that are
painted white, and a sheet-iron roof
the rain drums on. A fan blows warm air
beneath our feet to disperse the smell
of chicken-shit and, on dull days,
fluorescent lighting sees us.

You can tell me: if you come by
the North door, I am in the twelfth pen
on the left-hand side of the third row
from the floor; and in that pen
I am usually the middle one of three.
But, even without directions, you'd
discover me. I have the same orange-
red comb, yellow peak and auburn
feathers, but as the door opens and you
hear above the electric fan a kind of
one-word wail, I am the one
who sounds loudest in my head.

Listen. Outside this house there's an
orchard with small moss-green apple
trees; beyond that, two fields of
cabbages; then, on the far side of
the road, a broiler house. Listen:

one cockerel grows out of there, as
tall and proud as the first hour of sun.
Sometimes I stop calling with the others
to listen, and wonder if he hears me.

The next time you come here, look for me.
Notice the way I sound inside my head.
God made us all quite differently.
and blessed us with this expensive home.

Edwin Brock

▶ Is the poet writing only about hens, or about humans too?

Studying one poet

There are at least three ways to choose a poet to study.

You can use an anthology of poems by different poets, and see
which poems appeal to you. You then use the poet's name as a
starting-point for finding more poems by her or him.

Or you may already know a poet that you like, and you can start
immediately on reading more of that poet's work.

Or you can consult your teacher or librarian to get some
suggestions to start you off.

Here are some possible choices:

W. H. Auden	Robert Graves
James Berry	Thomas Hardy
John Betjeman	Tony Harrison
Edward Brathwaite	Seamus Heaney
Charles Causley	Ted Hughes
e. e. cummings	Elizabeth Jennings
Walter de la Mare	Linton Kwesi Johnson
Emily Dickinson	Philip Larkin
Carol Ann Duffy	D. H. Lawrence
Robert Frost	Liz Lockhead

Louis MacNeice
Roger McGough
Adrian Mitchell
Edwin Morgan
Wilfred Owen
Brian Patten
Ruth Pitter
Sylvia Plath
Kathleen Raine
James Reeves

Michael Rosen
Carl Sandburg
Siegfried Sassoon
Vernon Scannell
Stevie Smith
Edward Thomas
Derek Walcott
Judith Wright
Kit Wright

Don't feel obliged to choose from this list. You might find poets, men
and women, who have just been published for the first time and who
interest you.

Getting started

This is a checklist of activities to help you do a study of the poet you
have chosen. You should choose which activities suit you, and your
poet, best.

(a) Of all the poems you read, pick the two you enjoy most and say
why.

(b) Have the poems got anything in common — apart from being
written by the same person? Are there themes or topics or issues
which seem to be of particular interest to your poet? Does your
poet seem fond of writing in particular ways or of using
particular images?

(c) If your poet is alive, write to him or her, via the publisher of the
most recent book of theirs you can find. Keep a copy of your
letter. What are you going to write about?

(d) Prepare a short talk — say five minutes — for your class on your
poet. Alternatively, you could prepare it as a radio broadcast. It
should include:
  ▶ your feelings about the poems
  ▶ a reading aloud of at least one poem
  ▶ some details of the poet's life, if any are available.

(e) 'Poem to . . .' Write a poem of your own dedicated to your poet. It
could be about what one particular poem has made you feel or
think of. Or about several things which interest you about your
poet's work.

The Incident

Do you have any idea what it is like to be racially abused because you belong to a minority group? Farrukh Dhondy, who has lived and taught in England for many years, writes about this kind of experience in his story 'KBW'. The Habib family live in London but the incidents described here could happen anywhere. The title may puzzle you but all will be revealed. Now read on.

KBW

Tahir's gone now. No one to play chess with. I ask my dad for a game and he says he has a union meeting to attend this evening. 'Young Habib would've given you three in a row with one hand tied behind his blooming back,' he says as he goes out.

My dad says they're going to move an Irish family in. He knows that I shall miss Tahir. 'Maybe young Paddy will know some chess,' he says.

Their flat was exactly like ours, except the other way round, like when you see a thing in a mirror. Like twins growing out of each other our two flats were. And I was Tahir's best friend. The windows are still smashed, but the flat's been boarded up, like some others on our estate. It goes for kilometres. You must of heard of it, it's called the Devonmount estate, Borough of Hackney. I shan't go to cricket practice today. I dropped out after Tahir left. We joined the team together so I think it's only right that we pull out together.

My mother don't understand. She says, 'Go on out and do something. Go and play cricket, you can't help the way the world is. Don't sit there looking like a month of wet Sundays.'

Dad understands. 'Son, you're right. Don't have no truck with racialist swine.' He always talks like that. Mum still needles him about being a Communist and he always replies that he's a Red in her bed, and the day she tries to put him under for his political views, he'll leave. They all know my dad on the estate. Twenty-two years he's been here.

I was born here and went to school here, to Devonmount Juniors and then Devonmount Comprehensive, no less. Tahir came here eight months ago. His dad came from Bangladesh, because they were driven out by the riots. That's what Tahir told me. He came straight into the fourth form. I took him to school the first day. My dad introduced hisself to Mr Habib as

soon as they moved in, and he said to me at dinner that day, 'My boy, a Bengali family has moved in next door, and I've told mister that you are going to take master to school. He's in your school and I want you to take him in and stick him outside the headmaster's office.'

That's how I met Tahir. I asked him what games he liked and he said cricket so I took him to Mr Hadley, the local vicar who runs the cricket team, and Tahir bowled for us. He was great. He lit up when they said they wanted to try him. Mr Hadley gave him the bat and bowled to him, and Tahir struck it hard to mid-off and was caught first go. Then Hadley gave him the ball. Tahir stroked it like it was a pigeon or something and when he looked up there was a shine in his eyes, same as you get out of the toe of a shoe when you put spit on the leather. He took a short run and bowled that ball. It spun at an amazing speed to leg-side.

'What do we have here?' Mr Hadley said, and his glasses gleamed. Tahir was our best spin bowler. He took four wickets in the match against the Mercer's Estate. When we won that match we were sure to get to the finals with the Atlanta Atlases. They were the best estate club going. If we beat them we'd be champs of Hackney. If you don't live in Hackney and don't live on the Devonmount, you don't know what that means. But I'll tell you what it means. It means Vietnam, North Vietnam that is, beating America in a war. That's what it means, a little country with a lot of determination, and without two ha'pennies to rub together, beating what my dad calls the biggest military machine ever built by man or money. Because ours is the worst estate. The flats are filthy and the stairs and the courtyards are never cleaned. There's coal dumps in the yards and half the places are boarded up. You should have seen the Habibs' flat. Water pouring down the wall of one bedroom, the wallpaper peeling off like scabs, and the roof-plaster all torn to bits. My dad said that it was nothing less than a crying shame for a workers' government to treat the workers so. My mum said she remembered when she was a little girl, and they ought to be thankful for a bathful of water which was hot.

The door of their flat has been forced open and the young ones play in there. That's what they call kids who still go to primary school on the Devonmount. I'm not a little 'un any more, I'm twelve and I'm not interested in climbing the garbage carts and pulling bits off people's cars and playing cowboys and Indians or hide and seek or cops and robbers in the empty flats. I used to be, and in those days I couldn't see why everyone on the estate complained about it. To me the empty flats were space. They gave you the feeling not that you belonged there, but that the place belonged to you so you could never leave it. Last year they built an adventure playground for the little 'uns on an empty site, and they went in hordes there, but after a while they didn't like it, they stopped going and started back in the empty flats again. There was nothing to nick in the adventure playground but the empties. You can find and flog all-sorts of things around here. There are some blokes on the estate who'll give you quite a few pence for a load of pipes or even for boards and doorknobs and toilet seats and that, and the kids on the estate break in and rip everything up. It's only when a flat has been completely ripped up that it becomes a place to play in. It gets cleaned out like a corpse gutted by sharks. I walked through their flat yesterday and it's been done over.

When Tahir's family first moved in, the people around didn't like it. They didn't go to the trouble to worry them, but the boys from C Block came to our building and painted 'Niggers Out' on the landing. My dad said it was a shame and he gave me some turps and a rag and asked me to clean it off, but I couldn't, it wouldn't come off. He said it was an insult to coloureds, and I know it was because the lads from C Block don't like coloured people — they're always picking on Pakis and coons when they're in a gang. My mum says they only do it because they're really scared of them, but I don't think they are. When Tahir and I came home from school together they used to shout, 'Want to buy an elephant?' and all that bollocks. Tahir never took any notice. He always walked looking straight ahead, but even though he didn't understand what they were saying, he'd become very silent and not say a word to me all the rest of the way. I still think I was his best friend. There was always six of them and they was bigger than us. Sometimes they'd even come to our block and shout from downstairs. If Tahir's father heard them he'd come out on the gallery and shout back at them. I think he was a very brave man. He wasn't scared of anyone and he'd say, 'Get out, swine,' because those were the only swear words in English that he knew. He didn't speak English very much and when my dad met him on the stairs or invited him round for a cup of tea, he'd just say, 'It is very kind, don't trouble, please don't trouble.' Tahir told me once that his father was a karate expert and could break three bricks with one hand. And he was strong. One day when I was in their flat, he lifted a whole big refrigerator all by hisself from the bottom of the stairs.

The trouble all started with the newspapers. There was a story in the *Sun* one day which said that two people in London had died of typhoid. My mum and dad talked about it at home and Mrs Biggles, my mum's mate, said that a girl in C Block had been taken to St Margaret's Hospital and was under observation there. The girl was called Jenny and we knew her 'cause she used to go to the same school as my little sister Lynn.

The story went around the estate that there was typhus in the East End, and everybody was talking about it. Then a funny thing happened. We play cricket down in Haggerston Park and after the game, when Mr Hadley has locked the kit away in the hut at the corner, he takes us all to the vicarage and he gives us bags of crisps and cups of cocoa, and lets us listen to his records. Well, this last Saturday, we had a lot of kids turn up for cricket practice. Usually there's only the team, about thirteen lads, but this time there was eighteen because Mr Hadley said we had to have proper trials for the juniors team. We all sat around while James and Mr Hadley made the cocoa. He peeped around the door and said, 'There's only seven mugs, so you'll have to share the cocoa.'

We said, 'Right ho, umpire,' because that's what he liked to be called. Sometimes he tells us, if he's feeling like talking about church, that vicars are umpires from God and that life is like a test match between good and evil. I think Mr Hadley explains things well, but I still don't believe in it. My dad says that Hadley should stick to cricket and not brainwash the team, because my dad's dead against the Christians. He's an atheist but our mum tells us not to take any notice of him, because she believes in God.

Anyway, on this Saturday, James brought in the cups of cocoa to the team and gave them to every second person, as two people had to share. We were sitting in a circle on the carpet and Nick was changing the records. Every now and then someone would get up and there'd be an argument about whether to have David Essex or the Slade on next. Tahir never said a word. He was holding his steaming cup of cocoa and you could see the gaps in his teeth when he smiled. The lads would ask him to whistle and he'd always try but he couldn't do it on account of the big gap in his front teeth.

Next to Tahir there was a boy called Alan, and when Tahir had taken a few sips of the cocoa after it had cooled, he passed it on to him. The rest of us were fighting for the mugs, just mucking about sort of, and eating crisps at the same time. I was watching this boy Alan, who had freckles and a thin face which looked scared most of the time, and I could see that he didn't want to take the cup from Tahir.

'Have it, I've finished,' Tahir said.

Alan said he didn't want any cocoa, so Tahir turned to try and give the mug back to James.

'Everyone's got one,' James said. 'They're sharing if they haven't.'

'You didn't get,' Tahir said, smiling upward at James.

'I'll share someone's,' James replied, but when Tahir tried to give him his cup, he said, 'No, that's all right, you have the rest, I'll get some later.'

Tahir put his cup down in the middle of the carpet. All the cocoa from the other mugs was finished, but no one wanted to pick up Tahir's mug. Then it struck me. Mr Hadley shouted from the kitchen that the milk was finished, and there was a sort of silence in the room.

Tahir was searching the other faces. 'Anybody could drink it,' he said.

Nobody picked up the mug. It stood on the carpet, not even half drunk. I looked at the others. A second before they'd been laughing and talking, but now there was only the sound of the record player. I think Tahir understood. I looked at Alan. He had a look on his face like a dog that's been whipped. The others were looking at him too.

'I don't want any,' he said.

Mr Hadley, his red face shining still with the sweat of the game, came in and said that it had been a damned hard selection and if we put in a bit of practice we could beat the Atlases. 'Fine cricket,' he said, and he rubbed his hands as usual. 'With fine weather it'll be finer.'

Tahir was silent on the way home. He kept looking at his feet as we walked, and he looked thinner and even smaller than he normally looked.

When I got home, Mrs Biggles was there in the kitchen. 'They suspect typhus, the girl's shaking with fever and the poor dear didn't even recognize her own mother,' she was saying. She was asking Lynn questions about the girl Jenny who was in hospital. 'It's not known here,' the doctor said to her mother, 'it's the foreigners have brought it in, that's for sure, from Istanbul and Pakistan and now from that Ugandan Asians' place. We've never had these things here,' he went on.

'It's the blacks bring these things in here . . .' she said.

My mum went dead silent. After Mrs Biggles had left, my dad put his mug of tea on the table and said he didn't want Mrs Biggles and her filthy mouth in his house, but Mum pretended she didn't hear and kept looking at the telly screen.

Another odd thing happened, on the following Monday. I woke up and dressed for school. Usually by the time my cornflakes are on the table, Dad's gone to work, but I found him in the kitchen that morning. He looked worried. He was sitting at the kitchen table with his hair brushed back and shiny with hair oil. He was talking to Mum, and then he took his coat and left. Mum said the people on the estate were rats and they needed poisoning, or leastways they deserved it. 'He took him to the pub once,' she said, 'just once as far as I know.'

'Who?' I asked.

'That Mr Habib from next door, your Tahir's father, even though the poor man couldn't drink on account of his religion, he had to drag him along just to show everyone.'

'Who took him?'

'Them people from C,' she said, 'they've painted things on our door. I wish Dad would call the police.'

As I walked out to school I turned to the door and it said 'K B W' in big black letters.

Dad was furious with Mum for telling me about it, and they had a right row that evening. Mum had scrubbed it off the door with sandpaper.

'Did you come back with Tahir?' she asked.

Tahir had been at school that day, but he behaved a bit strange. He wasn't there for the last lesson and I reckoned he must have hopped it.

'What does it mean?' I asked my dad, remembering the letters.

'It means your dad is poking his nose into other people's business,' my mum said.

'You know what they painted on our door, son?' my dad asked.

'I saw it,' I said.

'It means Keep Britain White,' Dad said. He looked grey in the face and serious. 'You know what that means, son. It used to be the Jews in the thirties, now it's bleedin' Indians and Pakistanis. Some people have seen you with Tahir.'

'More like they've seen you chatting like old friends to Habash, or whatever his name is,' Mum said.

'I've seen a lot of it and I hoped you wouldn't grow up in a world with these anti-working-class prejudices. I don't care what your mum says, but we've got to fight it. I've been fighting it, and I hope my son and grandson will fight it too.'

'And a lot of good it's done you,' Mum said.

But I was kind of proud of my dad.

'They are fascist scum, lad,' he said. He always calls me 'lad' when he gets to lecturing about his politics.

'Don't go putting your ideas into the boy's head, you leave him to think as he pleases.'

Dad ignored her. He sat with his palms on his knees and with his tall back pushed against the chair, the way he always did when he thought he was teaching me the facts of life.

'You know this typhoid, lad,' he said. 'People are blaming the Habibs for bringing it in. But any law court in this country knows they're innocent. It's ignorance and superstition. This girl Jenny went to Spain on the school trip with our Lynn, didn't she?' This was said more to Mum than to me.

I hardly slept at all that night. The next day the papers said that the girl Jenny was worse and that several cases of typhoid had been found and more people had been put under observation in the East End hospitals. I was thinking that I knew why the cricket team hadn't wanted to touch Tahir's cocoa. I was wishing I had picked it up. I knew that Tahir must be thinking the same thing too. It struck me that he must have thought that I had the same idea as the rest of them.

Sometimes I have funny dreams and that's when I can't sleep. That night I dreamt of the letters K B W painted up across our door, and then the letters spread out with other letters on to the whole of the estate, and the letters growing and becoming bigger and bigger till they were too heavy and had to come crashing down, falling on top of me, the K like two great legs and the W spinning round like giant compasses.

I went very tired to school. I didn't tell Mum about the dream. Tahir wasn't in the playground and he wasn't at registration. I thought he might be late, but he never came late, and then it struck me that I knew he wouldn't come to school that day.

I stayed in that night and so did Dad. He usually goes down the pub for a jar, but he didn't bother that night. He turned on the telly and I could see from the way he folded his legs, and from his eyes which were glued on the screen but not taking in the programme, that he was worried. He usually starts on at Lynn when he's like that, asks her to polish her shoes for school the next day and for her homework and everything. It felt to me too as though something was about to happen, and it did.

I heard the crash and then another thud and another crash of glass and a woman screaming. It was Tahir's mother. Dad sprang up from his chair. I felt that he had been expecting it. He rushed to the door. Mum came out of the kitchen. The crash of brick or stone sounded as though it was in our own house. Dad opened the door and went out on to the gallery.

'Bastard, cowards!' I heard. It was Mr Habib shouting his lungs out.

Dad rushed back into the flat. 'There's twenty of them out there.'

'Shall I call the police?' Mum asked.

Dad didn't answer. Everyone hates coppers on our estate, and no one ever calls them. Coppers don't need invitations. I could hear the blokes downstairs shouting. Mum pushed Lynn away from her and went out on to the gallery.

Mr Habib was still shouting, 'You are all bastards, white bastards.'

Then we heard the running steps on the stairs. The blokes were coming up, and they were shouting too: 'Paki filth,' and, 'The girl's dead.'

It was all hell. Mr Habib went in and got Tahir's cricket bat. The blokes from C Block had bottles. There was more crashing of glass and Mrs Habib kept screaming things in Indian and I could hear Tahir crying and shouting and a lot of thumping.

'Why don't you help him?' my mum shouted to Dad. 'What kind of bloody Communist are you?' But Dad was pushing her into the kitchen.

'Shut your mouth,' he said to her. He never talks like that normally, but he looked as though he'd pissed himself. 'Let the police handle this. There's twenty of them out there.'

By the time the police came, with sirens blaring, pulling into the courtyard, jumping out and slamming their car doors, the blokes were gone.

I said, 'Mum I'm going out,' and before she could stop me I went to the door and unbolted it. Other people had come out of their flats. The galleries of all the floors were now full of people trying to see what had happened. The police called an ambulance, and they took Mr Habib, who was lying outside his door groaning, to hospital. Tahir was bending over him when the coppers came with an Indian bloke and started asking questions. Tahir looked up at me as I stepped out, and he looked away. His dad had all blood streaming down his face. The day after, the blood marks were still there, all over the gallery.

Two hours later, we were all still awake. It was still as death outside and silent.

'I'll take it up with the council,' my dad said. I knew what he felt. He had wanted to help Tahir's dad, I am sure, but he felt helpless. There were too many of the others, he couldn't have said nothing.

'I wouldn't be seen dead at that girl's funeral,' Dad said after a while.

Four Indian blokes came and took Tahir and his mum and all their stuff away that same night and we could hear the coppers who'd stayed behind arguing with them.

The next day at cricket Mr Hadley asked me where Tahir was. The other boys told him the whole story, that bricks had been thrown through their windows and that Tahir's dad was in hospital.

Mr Hadley knew our school and he turned up there the next day. The Headmaster sent for Tahir and for me from class and we walked together to the office without a word. Mr Hadley was there. He said he was sorry to hear that Tahir's family had been in an unfortunate incident and that he wanted Tahir to come to cricket practice.

Tahir answered all his questions about where they were living and that. He said, 'Yes, sir,' when Mr Hadley said that he must realize that he had a lot of good friends like me and that wherever he lived he must continue to play for Devonmount. He said, 'Yes, sir,' his legs apart, his hands folded behind his back, his head bent and his lips tight together, his eyes moving from Mr Hadley's face to the floor. But he never came again.

Farrukh Dhondy

Looking back

These suggestions for discussion, and possibly writing, are designed to take you back into the story to consider some of the issues involved.

Decide which three statements seem most important to you after reading the story:
▶ Tahir was a good cricketer.
▶ Bad housing can create bad feeling between races.
▶ The narrator's father should have helped Tahir's father when they were attacked.
▶ People were wrong to blame Tahir's family.
▶ The way newspapers report things can cause trouble.
▶ The narrator should have drunk from the cup Tahir used.
▶ The author wrote this story to show what racial prejudice is like.
▶ Tahir should have carried on playing cricket.

Who in the story attracts most sympathy for you?

What could the narrator, and his parents, have done to help Tahir's family?

Is the story completely pessimistic? Are there any optimistic clues?

Can a story change your opinion? Has this story had any effect on you?

Finally, you could write a version of part or the whole of this story from Tahir's point of view.

Racism is not always as physically violent and as obvious as in 'KBW'.

The second part of this unit deals with a situation that *could* happen in a school, and *could* be left to pass almost unnoticed, except by the people directly involved.

Keeping the issues of 'KBW' in mind, you're asked in this section to contribute to a story yourself. The situation is fictional, but you may find yourself discussing real-life incidents and attitudes as you go along.

The following extract was written by a fourteen-year-old girl. Her class was asked by their English teacher to do some autobiographical writing for a class booklet called *Our Lives So Far*.

My Life So Far

My name is Sita. I have lived in England all my life, moving many times because my father is a doctor and has worked in many different hospitals. My mother does not work but she is studying hard at college to get English qualifications. She already has a Science degree from an Indian University. At home we joke about the fact that if I were a bit older we could be doing exams together this Summer. On the whole I am very happy in England. After all it is my country and I haven't even visited India yet. Unfortunately some people assume because of my appearance and culture I do not belong here.

I think I must have been to four or five primary schools and it was always difficult to make new friends and get used to different teachers and different rules. Nearly always I had to put up with some abuse. Whenever I went into a classroom for the first time I was always tensed up and expecting the worst. Sometimes there was just an awkward atmosphere and hardly anyone would speak to me on the first day. The worst thing would be if the teacher asked one of the kids to look after me. By the time I was eight I had learned to keep to myself and wait for the other kids to try and make friends. At the worst school there was one boy who kept picking on me. He did everything from calling me names to spoiling my work, hiding my things and slyly kicking me under the table. Fortunately the teacher noticed and he got into trouble. It didn't make my life any easier because half the class ganged up with him but at least some kids sided with me and I made some friends.

When I tell my parents they tell me different things. My Mum says I should stand up for myself and report things but my Dad says it's bound to happen and I should try to avoid trouble as much as possible. My Mum said she wanted to come up to school but my Dad said leave it. Teachers do their best but they can't be everywhere. They've got this new anti-racist policy in my present school so it will be interesting to see if there is any change when things happen.

While reading through Sita's English work-book Tom Panton, her English teacher, notices racist comments scrawled in the margin of her latest piece of work. He sends this note to Jenny Hall, Sita's tutor, and a copy to Viv Manyan, the Head of House.

14 March

To: Jenny
From: Tom

What's happened to Sita? I noticed she wasn't in my lesson today. Someone's been scrawling graffiti on her work; must have happened yesterday when the work was left on my table at the end of period 3. I noticed Michelle and Sue in the room when I went past at lunchtime, before I picked up the folders. Could you find them and send them to me please at 11.30. I'm free then. I'll see if I can find out what's going on.

Tom

On the same day the headteacher receives a letter from Mrs Patel which explains why Sita is not in school.

14th March

Dear Mr Cross,

My daughter, Sita, came home from school today in a very distressed state. She told me that somebody in her class had deliberately written racist comments on her work. But she is unwilling to say who it is. She is far too upset to come back to school until something is done about this. Could you please telephone me at home this evening to arrange when I can come in to discuss this with you.

Yours sincerely

Amina Patel

Meanwhile, the rest of 4BS have been discussing the incident even though at this stage nothing official has been mentioned to them. But like most kids they know what's been going on. Below is part of the conversation they have at lunchtime on the day Sita hasn't turned up for school. Michelle and Sue are not present.

JOE: I feel really bad about it but what can we do?
LIZZIE: She did ask for it. I mean, she never tries to mix with the rest of us.
PAT: Well would you? We haven't exactly made her welcome, have we?
JOE: I don't like the way it looks as if we feel the same as those two.
PAT: How do you know it was them?
JOE: Course it was them. It's obvious. They've been getting at her ever since she came . . .

Dialogue

Continue the conversation as a play. You can bring in other members of Sita's class if you like. It can either be improvised and tape-recorded or written as a playscript.

Mr Cross, the Headteacher, passes on Mrs Patel's letter to Viv Manyan, Sita's Head of House. That evening Mrs Manyan phones up Mrs Patel and arranges an appointment for Wednesday 16 March. She will come in at 9 o'clock with Sita to talk about what has happened.

The interview

Reconstruct the interview between Mrs Patel, Sita, and Viv Manyan. Again this can be a tape-recording, an improvisation, or a playscript.

Having spoken to both Viv Manyan and Tom Panton, the headteacher is certain that Sue and Michelle were responsible for the racist comments on Sita's book, and realises that they have been unpleasant to her on previous occasions. He sends a letter to their parents explaining that the two girls are being sent home and making appointments to see their parents and the girls at 11 a.m. on Friday 18 March, two days later.

Letter-writing

Write the letter sent by the Head to one of the girls' parents. You can make up the address of the school and the girl's address.

The incident has now been dealt with and Michelle and Sue are back in school. Sita will be returning in the afternoon.

In your groups discuss each of the following:

(a) The headteacher writes a letter to Mr and Mrs Patel to explain what he has done. What does he include in it?

(b) Jenny Hall talks to the whole class at registration. What does she say to them?

(c) Some of the class decide they should make Sita more welcome. What do they decide to do?

(d) Michelle and Sue are having a conversation at lunchtime with Joe, Lizzie and Pat. What do they talk about?

Keep the notes you make during these discussions for the final reconstruction.

You now have a collection of writing which includes short play-scenes, letters, and discussion notes. Using these and the plan below, put together a class or group folder which reconstructs the whole incident. Many of the scenes shown on the plan are new but all of them are based on the writing and discussion you have already done. Be selective. You may not be able to cover every scene but make sure you cover the incident from beginning to end.

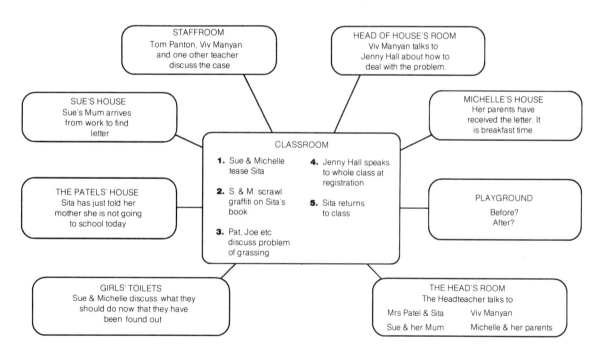

ADVICE

DEVELOPING YOUR WRITTEN WORK

This section has an outline of two ways that you can use to improve your writing. These are methods that are used by everyone who has to write anything important — and although they make the process of writing a bit longer, they will improve the quality of what you write.

If you're going to be writing alone and in a fixed length of time, as in an exam, then these methods will be of limited use. But if your writing is for a coursework folder there's time for you to use them.

Redrafting

Many people think that professional writers — authors, journalists, for example — just write down what they want to neatly and correctly first time. This is not true. Usually they write down quickly what they are thinking, in rough. This is called a first draft.

Then they go back and look at it again, changing words and sentences they don't like and correcting mistakes — which we all make when we are writing quickly. Having revised the first draft, they then write out a second draft, neater and better than the first.

Anything like a poem, a letter, or an essay that needs to be carefully presented will look better if you concentrate on getting your thoughts down first, and *then* worry about the mistakes, the handwriting, the crossings out, later.

Collaboration: redrafting ideas

Collaboration simply means working with someone else. In your GCSE course you can work with:

(a) other people in your class

Your friends will also be working on the same or similar tasks and can be 'readers' for your writing.

How can they help you?
They could help you with your spelling and punctuation — but that means they are looking only for mistakes, and many of those you

could spot for yourself. This is not the best way to collaborate.

The most valuable advice you can get is whether or not your 'reader' is satisfied with what you've written. Is your opinion clearly and logically expressed in your essay? Are your thoughts in a logical order? Is the opening of your story interesting enough? Do the characters need more description? Have you used the right tone and style for the purpose you intend for your piece?

In other words, have you done enough thinking, and are your ideas expressed in enough detail to help the reader be interested in what you're saying?

This kind of collaboration can happen at any point from the 'what shall I do?' planning stage through to your final draft.

Of course, you should do the same for them!

(b) your teacher

Your teacher would rather make suggestions about how a first draft could be improved than receive a fully finished piece of work that isn't as good as it could be. Chatting over the details of an idea isn't cheating — it's the way we all need to behave in order to help us get clear what's in our minds.

Proof-reading

If you've made a first draft and discussed it to help sort out your ideas, then you're probably already working on all those other things which make life easier for your reader:
▶ spelling
▶ punctuation
▶ paragraphing
▶ mistakes in word order
▶ the quality of vocabulary and expression.

Checking for mistakes, clearing up misunderstandings, and polishing up 'in best' is an irritating job. Proof-reading is the name given to this process by the professionals at the final stage before their work is printed. It is a different kind of redrafting from collaboration, though it could be part of it.

Your reader shouldn't have to struggle to decipher what you've written. If she or he does have to struggle then they quickly lose interest in the important things you're trying to communicate.

When you think of all the time you've spent working out what you want to say, it would be a pity to weaken it by not spending fifteen or twenty minutes extra when you are producing your final draft.

This chart is a simple plan to remind you what to look for in the final stages of writing your piece.

PROOF-READING — HOW DOES IT WORK?

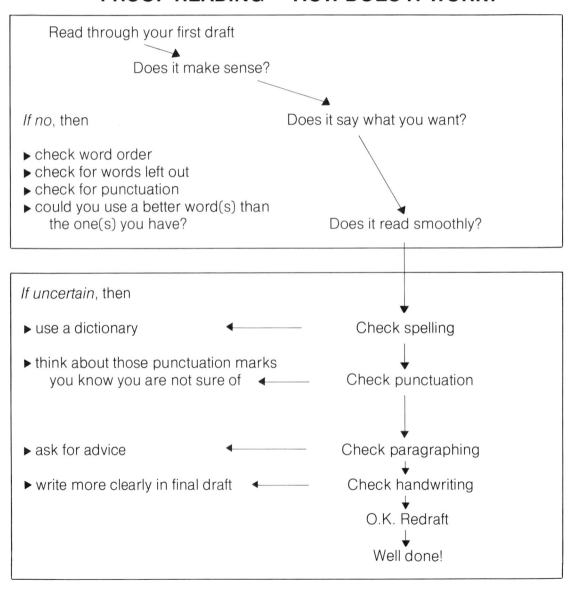

Read through your first draft

Does it make sense?

If *no*, then   Does it say what you want?

▶ check word order
▶ check for words left out
▶ check for punctuation
▶ could you use a better word(s) than
   the one(s) you have?   Does it read smoothly?

If uncertain, then

▶ use a dictionary   ←————— Check spelling

▶ think about those punctuation marks
   you know you are not sure of ←——— Check punctuation

▶ ask for advice   ←————— Check paragraphing

▶ write more clearly in final draft ←——— Check handwriting

O.K. Redraft

Well done!